SENADO

£14.99

C000171656

THE VOICES OF MACAO STONES

This book is dedicated to the memory of Sir Lindsay and Lady May Ride.

Foreigners in a foreign land, they both contributed much to Hong Kong,
and considered the place their home. Both also loved and understood Macao —
its past, its heritage, and its people. This book is a testament to that love and understanding.

JW
Hong Kong
1999

For Charlotte,

with every good wish,

[signature]

26/10/51

THE VOICES OF MACAO STONES

—❦—

Lindsay and May Ride

Abridged with additional material
by Jason Wordie

[signature]

Foreword

by John King Fairbank

香港大學出版社
HONG KONG UNIVERSITY PRESS

Hong Kong University Press
14/F Hing Wai Centre
7 Tin Wan Praya Road
Aberdeen
Hong Kong

© Hong Kong University Press 1999

ISBN 962 209 487 2

All rights reserved. No portion of this publication may
be reproduced or transmitted in any form or by any recording,
or any information storage or retrieval system, without permission
in writing from the publisher.

Printed in Hong Kong by Liang Yu Printing Factory Ltd.

Contents

STONES, ECCLESIASTICAL AND SECULAR

List of Illustrations

❧❦❧

After p. 126

PHOTOGRAPHS

MAP

Foreword

THE CHINESE LODESTONE has attracted foreigners from the earliest times, yet the country has ordinarily been so self-sufficient that its governments have kept foreigners quarantined on the borders. For the Westerners who came by sea after 1513, Macao became the chief frontier post, as Hong Kong still is today. Macao after 1557 and Hong Kong after 1841 played the role for seafarers that Kiakhta played after 1728 for those travellers who approached China by land, via Siberia.

Sir Lindsay and Lady Ride have recounted how a casual pastime, looking at inscriptions, developed into an avocation, began to occupy their travels on leave, and finally produced not one book but several. The Old Protestant Cemetery, one key to Macao, led them on to the monuments of the colony itself, described in this volume. But the colony of Macao was of course the precursor, indeed progenitor, of the colony of Hong Kong, the scene of Sir Lindsay's academic, official and military careers. His interest in researching the past has thus steadily broadened, without ever leaving home.

As all genealogists know, antiquarianism is its own reward. For the social scientist intent on ordered analysis, it can be a welcome relief. Instead of selecting data according to categories leading to conclusions, the antiquarian puts himself at the disposal of the data, uncovering the record for its own sake. An historian of course is part social scientist, part antiquarian, mixed according to taste. As historian-antiquarians, the Rides have used the solid three dimensional stones of Macao for work literally in the fourth dimension, to go back in time and see the origins, trace the persistence, of these monuments, and discover the people who made them. The result is a vivid impression of Macao's international past.

Sir Lindsay Ride's whole career has contributed to this current interest. Born in Victoria in 1898, he was schooled in Melbourne before going to Oxford as a Rhodes Scholar in 1922. Australia, though part of the New World, is nevertheless within the periphery of old China's attraction. After studying life at New College and rowing at Henley, he studied medicine at Guy's Hospital, London, and by 1928 was Professor of Physiology at the

University of Hong Kong. Two decades later, he began his great contribution there as Vice-Chancellor from 1949 to 1965.

Lindsay Ride was not only an athlete but a soldier who served in the Australian forces 1916–1919 and indeed was twice wounded. After the Japanese seizure of Hong Kong in 1941, he escaped to the mainland and soon organized and commanded the British Army Aid Group, an agency headquartered in Kweilin that kept track on events in Hong Kong, spirited people out and in, and in general prepared for whilst hastening the Japanese defeat. Colonel Ride's leadership of the B.A.A.G. was very impressive to me, as a young American official who visited Kweilin in the hot summer of 1943 in search of the war effort there. As far as I could see, he was it. After the war and while piloting the University through an era of revolution and uncertainty, Sir Lindsay also commanded the Hong Kong Volunteer Defence Force from 1948 to 1962.

His interest in Hong Kong's heritage, the men of all countries who have congregated on the China coast and mediated Sino-Western contact, thus comes from his immediate experience through five active decades. Now nominally retired, he and Lady Ride have quite naturally expanded their researches, but even when in office, Sir Lindsay was a part-time historian and published several basic contributions to the cultural history of the Macao-Hong Kong nexus. He has traced the origin of the University of Hong Kong up to 1911, and described the life work of two principal missionary sinologues, Robert Morrison, the pioneer translator of the Bible into Chinese, and James Legge, the pioneer translator of the Chinese Classics into English. It is in keeping with Sir Lindsay's broad theme that in successive generations Morrison accomplished his great work at Macao, and Legge at Hong Kong.

John K. Fairbank

This Foreword was written in November 1970, during the Rides' work on the project, by John K. Fairbank, then Francis Lee Higginson Professor of History, Harvard University.

Acknowledgements

THANKS FIRST AND FOREMOST must be made to the late Lady May Ride, who entrusted me with her and her husband's draft manuscript and research notes on the stones of Macao before retiring to England in 1996. She willingly assisted me at a distance in many practical and personal ways, and gave me complete freedom over the form the final volume was to take. The shape of the final work is mine, though heavily influenced by their earlier drafts. I hope that it remains something Sir Lindsay Ride would have recognized and approved of. Sadly, Lady May passed away in England the very day the manuscript of this book went to the Press.

Lady Ride wished to acknowledge the help given to her and her husband by the late Y.C. Liang, CBE in whose house they stayed in former years, and whose generosity in allowing them to do so many years ago enabled them to visit Macao for research and relaxation whenever they wished.

Lady Ride also wanted to make known the debt she and her husband owed to Monsignor Manuel Teixeira, doyen of Macao's historians. He greatly assisted the Rides over many years in their earlier stages of their research. The shape of the manuscript that I inherited, and the interest and enthusiasm for Macao, its heritage, parks and gardens and the stones themselves that it reflects, is a testament to the friendship that existed between the Rides, Monsignor Teixeira and the late Alfredo Alfonso da Almeida, of the Obras Públicas de Macau (Macao Public Works Department). He recognized the historical value of many of the old stones found all over Macao, rescued them from destruction, and helped to have many relocated and preserved for posterity.

Gloria D'Almada Barretto MBE first introduced me to Lady May Ride in 1995. Out of that introduction grew a warm friendship, transcending differences in age and personal experience, the memory of which I will always treasure. So to Gloria, for this and many other acts of help, kindness and hospitality over the years, my deep and grateful thanks.

The Instituto Cultural de Macau generously assisted with the costs of publication of this volume. They also provided a most helpful and timely financial subsidy to me, for which I remain deeply indebted and very grateful.

Dr Stanley Ho very generously provided, at Lady Ride's request, complimentary tickets on his Jetfoils which enabled me to travel to Macao for further research whenever I required. For this kindness, and the considerable practical help it afforded me, I remain thankful.

The staff at the Leal Senado de Macau have been most generous with both their time and resources. I would in particular like to thank Mr Alberto Cheang, for valuable assistance in obtaining permission to use some of the beautiful and evocative Smirnoff watercolours in their collection to illustrate this volume.

The staff at the National Library in Canberra, where the Braga Collection is housed, gave expert and ready assistance to this project during a research trip to that city.

Barbara Clarke, Dennis Cheung, Clara Ho and the staff of Hong Kong University Press have been unfailingly helpful and supportive throughout the long period this project has taken to reach publication.

The Reverend Carl T. Smith read an earlier draft of the Ride's papers, and then read my final manuscript again with great care and attention to detail. His keen eyes picked up numerous inaccuracies and shortcomings that I had overlooked. For his time, patience and scholarly generosity, my very sincere thanks.

Dr Peter Cunich of the University of Hong Kong has been of tremendous help to me in many practical ways, and has read a draft of the manuscript with great care and attention to detail. To Peter, and his wife Sarah, my very sincere thanks.

Michelle Wong of the History Department at the University of Hong Kong typed a very long section of manuscript onto disk for me, accurately and at great speed. Many thanks for her willing help and patience.

Ko Tim Keung has obligingly and with great skill taken a number of photographs to complement or replace some of the Ride's original pictures. For this and his many other acts of kindness and friendship to me in past years I remain very thankful.

David Ollerearnshaw read a draft of the manuscript, and made many constructive comments. By so doing he provided great insight into the requirements of the interested non-specialist reader. David, and his wife Evangeline, have also helped me in numerous practical ways during my work on this project. I am very grateful to them both for their patience and continued friendship to me.

Dr Elizabeth Sinn has been unfailingly encouraging and enthusiastic about the project from the time Lady Ride first passed the manuscripts and research notes to me in 1996.

Edward Stokes gave the type of encouragement and practical advice that only comes from being an established writer. For years of good counsel, always heard but not always heeded, my sincere thanks.

Vaudine England has been a source of solid advice, invaluable contacts and good-humoured friendship enjoyed over numerous pots of afternoon tea. Many thanks, for everything.

Bob and Jennifer Shepherd generously gave me free run of their home in England whenever I needed to be there. For their kindness, unstinting hospitality and continued friendship to me over many years I am very deeply appreciative.

Wee Kek Koon, at the final stage of my work on this book, gave everything a meaning and significance that I had never thought possible.

Jason Wordie
April 1999

Introduction

ONE MARCH EVENING in 1996, an old lady and a young man were dining together at Repulse Bay in Hong Kong. Talk somehow turned to Macao — which the old lady had loved since the days of her childhood in the 1920s, and the young man had turned to for relaxation and solace ever since he had first came to Hong Kong in the late 1980s.

Their conversation that evening spanned the whole length and breadth of Macao and its past — about the great Macanese hero Mesquita, and Ferreira do Amaral, the old forts, and the view from Guia, the graves in the Protestant Cemetery; they looked at pictures of old Macanese clothes, and talked about the people and culture of this most special and unlikely place. A shared love of Macao, one that touched on many different elements, transcended the generations and made immediate past experiences, as it has for many people over the centuries when they come to talk about Macao.

There was also an understanding between them, too, about the meaning and wider significance of Macao, that for so very long had stood as the only maritime window into the vastness of China. And a joint recognition that were it not for those earlier centuries spent upon the low ridge of hills, at the farthest extremity of the Chinese Empire, there would have been no Hong Kong either. It would have remained a remote and beautiful island, the haunt of fisherfolk and pirates, of no consequence except to the few hundred villagers who made their homes there. From Hong Kong talk returned, inevitably, back to the tiny Portuguese territory on the other side of the Delta where Hong Kong itself began — back to Macao.

The evening drew late, and the young man left to return to his home in the New Territories. Macao and the thought of it remained with him for hours afterwards, as contact with the place always does. It had been a very pleasant evening.

The very next night, when they happened to meet again at the annual dinner of the Hong Kong Branch of the Royal Asiatic Society, the old lady excitedly turned to the young man and said 'You must have the *Stones!*'

'What sort of *Stones?*', he thought to himself as he smiled politely and asked for further details, wondering at how he could carry such heavy things away and where they would fit when he got them home again.

The '*Stones*', it turned out, was the unpublished, incomplete work on the historical sites of Macao that the old lady and her husband had worked upon for many years. It sounded very interesting, and a worthwhile challenge. The young man thanked her and agreed to take up the work, and see it through to publication. That was in 1996.

The old lady was Lady May Ride, widow of Sir Lindsay Ride, founder and Commandant of the wartime British Army Aid Group in China, and for many years Vice-Chancellor of the University of Hong Kong.

The young man was me.

The Voices of Macao Stones, the book you are now reading, is the culmination of their work in Macao over many years.

In 1928 the newly-arrived Professor of Physiology at Hong Kong University, Lindsay Ride, visited Macao with the then Member of the Legislative Council representing the Portuguese community, J.P. Braga. This was the beginning of a half-century long association with the small Portuguese territory. Close geographically to Hong Kong, yet in many respects so remote in time and outlook, and with echoes still to be faintly heard of the founding of the British colony, little more than eighty years before.

The young professor was intrigued by the beauty of Macao and fascinated by the sense of history it still contained for him at almost every turn. Most of all he was captivated by the old Protestant Cemetery, then a picturesque ruin near the Grotto of Camões, and the engaging lives that its many gently decaying tombstones seemed to hint at. It was the beginning of an interest in and love for Macao that was to grow and continue for the rest of his life — and beyond, too, for his was ashes were interred there following his death in 1977.

His widow, May, began her association with the Portuguese colony at about the same time, as a visitor from neighbouring Hong Kong. Following their marriage in 1954, Macao became a place of refuge for them, as it had been for many in the course of the preceding centuries. For them, the respite was from the pressures of work and an increasingly busy public life, due to Ride's dual role as Vice-Chancellor of the University of Hong Kong and Brigadier-Commandant of the Hong Kong Volunteer Defence Force. These various pressures gradually diminished after Lindsay Ride's retirement from the University in 1964, but their love of Macao and interest in its past went on.

The genesis of this book began in 1954, but was diverted for a long period so that restoration and research on the Old Protestant Cemetery could be completed. In an early stage of its development it was finally halted — or so it seemed at the time — by the death of Sir Lindsay Ride in October 1977. Monsignor Manuel Teixiera utilized some of the material gathered by the Rides and himself in his own work on the stones, statues and memorials; *A Voz das Pedras de Macau* published in 1980. Some of the earlier research material was incorporated in *An East India Company Cemetery: Protestant Burials in Macao,* edited by the late Bernard Mellor and finally brought to publication in 1995.

Much painstaking research on the part of the Rides' had gone into both the early drafts of *The Voices of Macao Stones* and *An East India Company*

Cemetery: Protestant Burials in Macao. Much else remained, in boxes and filing cabinets, waiting to be taken apart, added to, edited and then put back together again. This has proved to be my main task, and the most time-consuming — though ultimately rewarding — part of the entire undertaking.

I have resisted the urge to go on and completely document every extant stone, statue, memorial plaque and marker that exists in present-day Macao. There are far too many of them; such a task would render any resulting book opaque to the general reader. The text is substantially as it was written in the 1970s before Sir Lindsay Ride's death. I have updated certain parts, edited and slightly altered others to improve overall flow, and where necessary added details of the later history of some of the *dramatis personae* in the story of Macao's stones. And so this book tells the story of Macao, by the medium of the stones left behind and scattered all over the little place like so many fragments of history. From the earliest days of Portuguese settlement near the old Ah-Ma Temple on the Inner Harbour, down to a statue erected to the victory over pirates at Coloane in 1910.

I have concentrated on telling, as the Rides themselves intended, a selective history of the oldest European settlement in China. Left behind as it has been by the tides and currents of history, it is the last remaining European colony in Asia. As is perhaps fitting, the Portuguese, whose toe-hold on this tiny place and significance in the history of the Far East greatly outweighs their contribution in later centuries, should be the last representatives of Imperial Europe to finally depart the stage.

Much of Macao's wonderful heritage — indeed far more than most casual visitors to the place ever realize — has been spared the blind destroying greed of the modern property developer. The timelessly beautiful banyan-lined curve of the Praia Grande has been lost in this way, and is no more, as Austin Coates described it in the 1960s, 'that elegant crescent of Latin architecture facing the waterfront, beyond which rise the low domes and towers of seminaries and churches, the whole creating that uniquely unexpected European view that is Macao's greeting to every visitor from the sea.' This element of Macao is lacking now, and has gone forever. Lost like the lost poems of Sappho, and wrecked as the English wrecked the Summer Palace in Peking, the Praia Grande only exists now in photographs and in the mind of the people who once walked along it. Those who remember the old and graceful curve, with muddy waves lapping at the edges of the sea-wall, and old men playing draughts under its venerable trees, and who loved it for what it was and for what it seemed to stand for, are right to mourn its loss.

Hidden away though, in odd corners or standing incongruous surrounded by modern buildings and thronged with traffic, un-noticed by almost all who pass, are the treasure-vaults of Macao's rich and colourful history. Of less immediate commercial value than the land along the Praia Grande, and so saved from wanton destruction, are other, more secluded relics.

In the cool shadows of old churches, set into the walls of long-disused fortresses, and in tranquil and leafy gardens, lie the silent stone keys that unlock the secrets of Macao and its opulent and varied past.

The retrocession of Macao to China in 1999 brings to a close nearly four hundred and fifty years of Portuguese control over this small and unlikely place. That part of this history should have been recorded by those who lived almost their entire lives in the nearby British Colony should not be surprising.

In its day Macao was of a richness and commercial position comparable in every way to Venice — as the late writer Austin Coates, himself an incomparable chronicler of Hong Kong and Macao once wrote, whichever city he was in, he somehow woke up in the morning wondering just which one it was. Macao still gives that feeling to its visitors.

Sometimes when I am staying over in Macao, I awake late at night and look out the windows across the city. Macao at night slows down, unlike urban Hong Kong, but never entirely stops. For a long time I stand and watch out from my room high above the town in the old Central Hotel on Avenida de Almeida Ribeiro where I generally stay, and the view is always the same. Yet, in some odd way, it feels subtly different every time I am there. The beam from the old lighthouse at Guia flashes past, drawing my eye to the floodlit ramparts of the centuries-old fortress on which it stands. Further over, the walls of The Monte, less brightly illuminated than Guia, loom darkly against the night sky. Before them, brightly highlighted, stand the ruins of St. Paul's Collegiate Church, the enduring symbol of Macao to so many, and its most popular tourist sight. In the darkness, it rears its empty façade heavenwards, its empty windows like so many sightless eyes, looking backwards to a golden age that passed its peak centuries before any of us now alive were even born.

At this hour, modern Macao becomes transformed and the changes of the recent past slip away. Along the darkened streets, away in the shadows, the stones in their hidden places take voice, and speak of a past richly peopled. Portuguese fidalgos, Jesuit priests, British merchants, Chinese mandarins, adventurers of every race and shade, all came together in this unlikely, remote corner of the world. For those with an ear to listen to their voices, of which Macao stones are an echo, still speak in soft tones, of times past, people long-dead, and an era and a way of thinking about the world that has gone for ever.

This quiet murmuring is the deep and real satisfaction of Macao, its best reason for coming, and one for which its stones provide a very necessary contemporary visual link. The joy of a visit to Macao, now more than ever before, is largely to be found in its past. Its monuments to the present day are often pedestrian, ugly and lacking in inspiration, built without heed to either their surroundings or their context; the beauties of the Macanese past subsumed into an often very tasteless, short-term and unfeeling now.

Comparisons between Hong Kong and Macao as regards architectural heritage are perhaps inevitable. As old photographs attest, they were both very similar once. Modern Hong Kong has lost almost all of what it once had, and in the process has also lost much of what it once was — for good and bad. It is gratifying to see, however, that Macao has followed the example of Singapore in terms of preservation; they have stopped themselves in time, for the most part at least, and are gradually developing an appreciation of their own past, in all its diverse complexity as a better guide to the present. In that, I would concur with the inscription on the tombstone of Sir Lindsay Ride in the Old Protestant Cemetery — *O Melhor Guia Futuro e O Passado* — the best guide to the future is the past.

Searching out the individual stones and

memorials, and discovering something of what has happened to those that are no longer still to be seen has been a time-consuming task, but it has been very worthwhile and rewarding. It has given me the opportunity to ramble and wander at will in Macao, a happy ambling pastime that I have never tired of yet.

And as with the Rides many years before me, I have always returned to my home in Hong Kong refreshed and renewed, by contact with the old and civilized stones — markers of the way which Macao in the course of its long history has taken and yet which still remain in place, as they always have been, ready to face the dawn of a new day.

Jason Wordie
April 1999

Ah-Ma Temple from the Braga Collection

To The Indies by George Smirnoff

Exterior view of the Leal Senado by George Smirnoff in 1945

Interior view of the Leal Senado by George Smirnoff

View of Macao and The Monte by George Smirnoff

View of the gatehouse of The Monte by George Smirnoff

View of the ramparts of The Monte by George Smirnoff

Inside The Monte by George Smirnoff

Portuguese Voyages of Discovery

THE PORTUGUESE CITY of Macao stands on a promontory jutting out, like a water-lily as one of its Chinese names describes it, from the south-east corner of the large delta island of Heung Shan (Fragrant Mountains) which forms the outermost part of the western lip of the Pearl River estuary. It is built on the shore of a small harbour, which geographical features divide into inner and outer portions. For many centuries this harbour has been chiefly the home of fisher-folk and a port for river, coastal and even deep-sea trade, but it has also always been a haven for any craft seeking either shelter from the storms of the South China Sea, or refuge from pirates — when it was not itself a pirate stronghold. The coming of the Portuguese led to an increase in its local and regional trade, and also to the establishment of a new intercontinental trade, as other European maritime powers followed Portugal's lead and made Macao the terminus of their Asian trade routes as well.

Much of Macao's early history can be gleaned from her temples, churches, and civic buildings, while the personal history of those who contributed to her establishment and development is preserved in her private memorials and public monuments. It is from these records in stone that we propose to reconstruct as much of the history of Macao and of her influence on the emergence of modern South-East Asia, as is necessary to enable readers to form their own opinions from the biographies in our later pages.

THE TEMPLE OF MA-KOK-MIU (媽閣廟)

THIS TEMPLE IS the building with which consideration of Macao's history should begin, both from the point of view of age and from the fact that it was from it that Macao derived its name.

The early boat people of south China, like most seafolk the world over, were highly religious, and invariably burned incense and made thank-offerings to their sea-goddess on their safe return from a successful venture afloat, or for their delivery from the dangers of any particularly perilous part of it.

Their *Notre Dame de la Garde* was Leung Ma (娘媽), one of the manifestations of T'ien Ho (天后), the Queen of Heaven, and shrines dedicated to her were to be found along the whole of the coast stretching from Fukien in the north-east, to far beyond Hainan in the south-west. Ma-Kok-Miu temple was one of these and it was built at about the end of the thirteenth century, according to some scholars, on the south-western tip of what is now the Macao promontory, just inside the rocky headland which separates the outer from the inner harbour. This is where, so legend has it, a Fukien trader was brought to safety by Leung Ma, who, in the form of a beautiful maiden, is supposed to have appeared on board his junk when it was in danger of sinking in a storm. This beautiful pilot steered the junk through the fury of the storm to the safety of a cove behind a rocky headland, thus saving the lives of all on board. It was not, however, until their rescuer went ashore and disappeared into the skies from the top of one of the nearby rocky outcrops that it was realized their benefactress was none other than the patron goddess of the Fukien boat people. Near this rock the trader built a shrine in her honour, and this later became the nucleus around which, by stages, the present temple was built. In it there used to be a model of a junk with the goddess at the helm; this no longer exists, but on rock faces nearby, there are numerous carvings of junks, reminders in stone of the event which led to the founding of the temple. Many centuries later, the Portuguese were to build their Barra Fort on this headland near the temple, and so, for centuries now, both have pointed the way to the haven beyond, the temple to boat-people seeking shelter from storms, the fort to those fleeing from the inhumanity of fellow men. Modern history has thus witnessed this haven change its name and its

nationality, but not its hospitable nature to which many members of a Hong Kong generation, only now growing old, can testify; they have cause to be ever grateful for the welcome and the hospitality which the people of Macao so freely — and with no little cost and danger to themselves — extended to those who sought refuge there from the terrors of the Japanese occupation of Hong Kong in 1941. It is estimated that during this period, the population of Macao rose at times to as much as 500 000, although it had normal accommodation and supplies for only 200 000 souls. This extra demand for food, medicines and the ordinary necessities of life had to come from Macao's own meagre resources, for although Japan did not occupy the Province militarily, she controlled all its lines of communication and therefore its imports. It was consequently not very easy for Macao to obtain extra supplies for those who had secretly fled from Japanese occupied territory. Even under these circumstances, no refugee of whatever race, creed or nationality was denied such hospitality as Macao could afford to give, and this was Macao's record too in 1937 when 170 000 Chinese fled there from Japanese-threatened Canton. May Macao ever remain a haven for the needy.

As the intimate and diminutive form of the name of the goddess Leung Ma was Ah-Ma, her temple naturally came to be called the Temple of Ah-Ma, and the nearby cove — now the Inner Harbour — became known as Ah-ma-(k)ao, meaning 'Ah-Ma Cove'; with this name in everyday use for the cove, it was inevitable that it should also be applied to the settlement that subsequently grew up on its eastern shore. The Temple of Ah-Ma which started this train of names is now known as Ma-Kok-Miu (媽閣廟) and its picturesque position and sprawling courtyards appeal to present-day visitors no less than its sanctuary catered for devotees from the seas in earlier eras.

IBERIAN MARITIME EXPANSION

PORTUGAL'S DISCOVERY of the long route round the Cape of Good Hope and the establishment of her sea-routes to the orient were made in many stages by a succession of adventurous navigators who, throughout their voyages, were continually harassed by their European rivals and constantly confronted by the opposition of the local rulers of territories through which they travelled. One by one these obstacles had to be overcome and the new positions consolidated before the next stage could be undertaken. Each such stage in this progression was a triumph in itself, accomplished as it was in uncharted seas, without chronometers or telescopes, and with only the simplest of navigational aids, and the most meagre resources of men, munitions and supplies which were all that the small craft of those days could carry.

These progressive stages were numerous and varied, as were the reasons why each in its turn was undertaken. But there was one basic reason which underlay the general plan of attempting to establish Portuguese trade with China: it was Portugal's reply to the challenge of Marco Polo overland route, which he had blazed from Venice to Cathay, after the final failure of the Crusades to establish a safe land route from the Levantine ports on the Mediterranean Sea to those on the Red Sea and the Persian Gulf. Polo's route brought little material advantage to the people of the Iberian peninsula who were too far to the west of the Venetian terminal market to benefit from it, so, if Spain and Portugal were to share in the riches of the orient, it had to be by other than the established overland routes. These two countries accepted this challenge by turning the defence of their peninsula against the ceaseless pounding of the Atlantic into attack. Their ships would plough their furrows through the ocean lanes and establish sea routes to the orient. But instead of the common heritage of these two countries uniting them against their common

The Temple of Ma-Kok-Miu: Showing here the rock carving of the legendary junk.(Courtesy of Dr Christina Cheng)

difficulties, these neighbours allowed their common aims to turn them into hereditary enemies. This enmity was counteracted to a certain extent by the Spanish belief that the quickest and surest sea approach to the orient was via the western Atlantic, while the explorations down the west coast of Africa led the Portuguese further and further south in the hope of discovering an eastern approach to the same goal. The success of these latter voyages prompted Prince Henry, 'The Navigator', to petition the Pope for the concession of all lands discovered by the Portuguese 'beyond Cape Bojador to the Indies inclusive, especially submitting to His Holiness that the salvation of these people [the natives of these newly discovered lands] was the principle object of his labours in that conquest'. This petition was successful and a Papal Bull was issued to this effect. This concession to the Portuguese was not to the liking of the Spanish, so they, after the first voyage of Christopher Columbus, made a similar petition to the Pope for a concession of lands discovered by them in the south and west of the Atlantic. This too was granted by a Bull (4 May 1493), but foreseeing that these allocations of areas would only lead to more and worse trouble between the two rival nations unless their zones were clearly delineated, the Pope laid down a Demarcation Line between them. This line ran along the whole length of the meridian of longitude drawn '100 leagues west of the Azores and Cape Verde Islands'.

There were a number of weaknesses inherent in the Papal plan that made it impracticable to implement it. In the first place, no such meridian could be drawn because the Azores and Cape Verde Islands were not on the same north and south line; secondly, the Spanish could not reach their zone without violating that of Portugal, and thirdly,

even if the plan had worked in the Atlantic, it only transferred and postponed the reconfrontation of these rival nations to a later date on the other side of this round world. But in addition, the Pope's line was strongly opposed by the then King of Portugal, who feared that it allowed the Spanish to approach too close to the west coast of Africa. His protests to Rome meeting with no response, he took the wisest course of proposing that the two interested parties should meet around a conference table and decide the matter for themselves. As a result, an agreement was reached and embodied in the Treaty of Tordesillas in 1494, but Papal approval was not granted until the Bull of 24 June 1506. By this agreement, the line of demarcation was shifted to the meridian situated 370 leagues west of the Cape Verde Islands; the treaty also gave the Spanish the right of navigation to and from their zone across that of Portugal. Its most important effect in the Atlantic was on the Americas; the line crossed the southern continent, dividing it so that Brazil came to lie mainly in the Portuguese sphere while the West Indies and the rest of South America were in the Spanish zone. It is this demarcation which accounts for the present-day distribution of the two Iberian influences and languages on that continent. But the most far-reaching and important effect of this Atlantic line was felt in the Pacific. This line enabled Magellan (a disgruntled Portuguese who had defected to Spain) to round The Horn from the Atlantic Spanish sphere and to open up Spanish trade from the eastern Pacific with the Spice Islands in the East Indies, and with the Philippines, Macao and Japan, where they met again their European neighbours and rivals.

The Portuguese, on the other hand, were free to develop the islands of the east Atlantic as staging posts and from these bases they eventually pushed their explorations round the Cape of Good Hope, whence the winds of the Indian Ocean fanned them out to the fringes of Afro-Asia; on those shores they built their trading settlements, which later were to form Portugal's empire in the orient. Thus while Spain was hewing her empire out of the seemingly limitless land mass of the American continents, Portugal was forming her maritime empire out of the numerous small settlement which she established on the shores of the large oriental oceans, stringing them on her long sea lanes like beads on a rosary. The simile of a rosary is apt, for throughout the establishment of their trade routes to China and Japan, religion was a major driving force with all Portugal's adventurers. All her pathfinders in their voyages of exploration went with the Vatican's blessing and, to no small extent, under its instructions; in addition, her priests went *with* the explorers and were not relegated to the status of flag followers, as was the case with later expeditions from Protestant countries. Vasco da Gama himself made this very clear when he stated that his dual reason for coming to India was 'Christians and spices'. As evidence of the importance of religion in the building of Portugal's empire, we need only cite the many churches and shrines, or their remains, which still lie along the routes of her expansion — and her regression; and of these memorials, Macao has excellent examples to show, both in the form of existing churches and of historic ruins.

ENGLISH ROYAL BLOOD

TO FOLLOW PORTUGAL'S overseas expansion from its beginning in the north Atlantic to its terminus on the shores of the China Seas, we must turn first to the late decades of the fourteenth century. This period witnessed the arrival on the Iberian peninsula from England of a Lancastrian duke, and the subsequent decades saw the infusion of English blood into Portuguese royal veins, a consequence which had not a little to do with Portugal's ultimate maritime development.

The English royal personage was John of Gaunt, the Duke of Lancaster, Edward III's fourth son, and in 1386 he landed at Santiago to lead an expedition against Spain in the belief that he was the rightful King of Castile. He was encouraged in this belief by his second wife, the ex-Infanta Constance, a daughter of ex-King Pedro the Cruel of Castile who had been dethroned and was later murdered. As was possible in those days, the Duke — who had already adopted the style of 'King of Castile and Leon' — took with him his Queen and his two daughters, and these, as we shall see, were in no way an encumbrance. The ladies played an important part in the preliminaries to the war, for John of Gaunt had no army to speak of and depended on persuading King John of Portugal to supply him with one for the invasion of Castile. The negotiations for this were based on the 1373 Treaty of Windsor in which England and Portugal agreed to help one another against all enemies, and the Duke of Lancaster's Castillian wife had much to do behind the scenes with the success of the negotiations. Part of the price paid to King John was the hand in marriage of Philippa, the Duke's elder daughter. She was the daughter of his first wife who was English, and thus in 1386 an English lady of royal blood became queen of Portugal.

John and Philippa had many children, among them being five sons who alternately were given English and Portuguese names. They have been described as 'a magnificent set of Infantes', extremely talented and greatly devoted to their mother who brought them all up both strictly and lovingly with their future duties to their country and its people always in mind. The eldest, named Edward after his grandfather Edward III of England, was a philosopher and succeeded to the throne of Portugal as Edward (Duarte) I (1433–1438); then came Pedro, a man of letters, followed by the greatest of them all, Henry, named after his English uncle. He was born in 1394 in the Rua dos Ingleses in Oporto and became one of the greatest figures in astronomical, geographical and navigational discovery of the fifteenth century. The other two sons were John who became the Constable of Portugal and the Grand Master of the Order of Santiago, and Ferdinand, a monastic who became the Master of Avis and the Martyr of Fez.

Their father, João I, was an able and enlightened ruler who, by his victories on land over the Moors and the Spanish, had established for himself and his heirs the Avis dynasty — the greatest in Portugal's history — and for his country, a leading status among Europe's western kingdoms. After a struggle lasting for about twenty years, King John felt his country was so firmly established at home that he could attack the Moors' lines of communications and bases overseas. He chose as his first objective Ceuta, the African port on the Straits of Gibraltar one of the main supply bases supporting the Moorish forces that were still occupying parts of the Iberian peninsula. This war thus acquired in the eyes of the Vatican and of many of the crowned heads of Europe, the status of a crusade, and it won the active support of many of them, including Henry V of England. Queen Philippa saw in it too a glorious and chivalric crusade and she readily supported the King in his decision for three of his sons, Edward, Pedro and Henry, to join the crusade.

By the year 1415, the Portuguese army and fleet were ready for the expedition but just before it was due to sail, Queen Philippa was stricken with the plague then raging in the Peninsula, and fearing lest her illness or death might delay the departure of the expedition or even pass the sickness on to the King, she persuaded him to leave and make his final preparations elsewhere. She then sent for her three sons and to each she presented a sword which she had had specially made for the occasion and to each she gave her blessing and also advice suited to their future lives.

To Edward, the heir to the throne, speaking of dealing with his subjects with justice and pity, she said:

> I give you this sword with my blessing and that of your grandparents from whom I descend. Though it be strange for knights to take swords from the hands of women, I ask you not to object, for because of my lineage and the will I have for the increase of your honour, I think no harm can come to you by it; nay, rather I believe that my blessing and that of my ancestors will be of great help to you.

To Pedro, having watched him from childhood honouring and serving women, she gave the charge of all 'ladies and damsels', but to Henry her favourite, speaking with the pride of a Plantagenet, she said:

> This one [his sword] I kept for you, for I think it is strong like yourself. To you I commend the lords, knights, fidalgos and squires it often happens that kings, owing to false information and unfair petitions from the people, take measures against them that they should not.

It is reported that even before the Queen finished speaking to her sons, the wind rose; on being told it was from the north which she knew was favourable for the expedition, she unselfishly said she hoped that they would set forth on the Feast of St. James which was due in the next few days. Queen Philippa did not live to see the magnificent spectacle of the fleet's departure, for she died the day after taking leave of her sons. A year after her temporary burial at Odivel los, her remains were reinterred in the 'English-looking Gothic Abbey' built at Batalha by King João to commemorate the Portuguese victory over the Spanish at the Battle of Aljabarrota on 14 August 1385. Here too the King's body was later laid to rest, and on their tomb, in the church which together they had watched being built, their stone figures also lie together, hand in hand.

King John's expedition against Ceuta was a complete success, but in addition, it was a source of personal satisfaction to him for his three sons all fought valiantly throughout the attack and were knighted on the field of battle for the valour they displayed during the capture of the city. But it was the younger brother Henry who really won his spurs there and as a result, in the courts throughout Europe his renown stood high and his name became a household word. On the other hand, these courts had no attraction for him. This was Edward's sphere and he toured them all, personally consolidating Portugal's newly won status among all the leading crowned heads of Europe. But from the victory at Ceuta, not only did the infusion of English Plantagenet blood in the Portuguese royal line emerge with flying colours, but so did the numerous English noblemen who took part in the crusade. Many of them remained in Portugal where they subsequently contributed much to the blending of these two seafaring races which helped the new

Portugal blossom into its fifteenth century maritime glory.

PRINCE HENRY, THE NAVIGATOR

MUCH OF THIS GLORY was due to the third son of John and Philippa, the studious and intelligent prince now known to history as Henry, the Navigator. He learned much more than methods of warfare from his experiences in the Ceuta expedition. He learned that most of the Moors' supply of gold came by overland caravans to Ceuta from the region of the headwaters of the Niger and Senegal rivers far to the south. On his return to Portugal, he eschewed all the usual social commitments of royalty, and, returning to the solitude of his observatory on the Cape of Sagres, he thoroughly immersed himself in the geographic, navigational, cartographic and astronomical problems that his plans for the exploration of the African Atlantic coast presented. He was made General of the Order of Christ and as such, was able to channel much of the enthusiasm and funds being misapplied on crusades, into the more useful fields of science and discovery. He devised navigational aids and trained officers in their use, and planned and dispatched expeditions down the north-west African coast as well as to the islands in the west Atlantic. Prince Henry studied the information that each of these relays of explorers brought back to him, and incorporated it in his plans for future explorations. He was certain that these explorations would ultimately lead to the discovery of the sea route to India, for he firmly believed that to the south of Africa there was a cape that would eventually be doubled by his explorers.

Prince Henry, however, did not live to see his

confidence confirmed. He died in 1460, but it was navigators of his school, brought up in his tradition, following his prophesying plans and using charts and maps drawn up by him forty years previously, who rounded the Cape of Good Hope and reached India by sea before the close of the fifteenth century. There remain only two reminders in Macao of Prince Henry's great achievement in preparing the way for Portugal's oriental empire — other than the existence of Macao itself — the street that bears his name, *Avenida do Infante Dom Henrique,* and a stone in front of the Liceu Nacional Dom Henrique, erected in 1960, five hundred years after his death.

Bust in the library of the Liceu Nacional Dom Henrique, commemorating Henry the Navigator, unveiled on 11 November 1960.

Macao street sign bearing the legend Avenida do Infante Dom Henrique.

PORTUGUESE EXPLORERS

PRINCE HENRY HIMSELF did not take part in any of these explorative adventures in the eastern Atlantic. This he left to those intrepid men of the sea more suited for that side of the work while he became the guiding scientific mind that planned and correlated all the expeditions that emanated from Portugal. It was his navigators who first explored the Madeiras in the years 1418–1420, although some of the islands had already been discovered by then.

In the late 1420s and the early 1430s, the Azores were discovered and explored by Diogo de Seville, but it took ten years of continued efforts to double Cape Bojador. This was eventually achieved in 1433–1434 by Gil Eanóes and thereafter exploration down the coast became much more rapid and much more lucrative. Gold and slaves in plenty were brought back to Portugal but the slave side of the trade was soon forbidden by Prince Henry. In 1444, his Ceuta dreams began to come true when Nuno Tristam reached the mouth of the Senegal River and when a year later, Dinnis Dias rounded Cape Verde. During the years 1455–1457, a Venetian — Alvise da Cadamosto — in the service of Prince Henry discovered the Cape Verde Islands and explored the Senegal and Gambia Rivers. With these explorations, practically the whole of Prince Henry's Ceuta dreams were fulfilled.

All these later voyages of exploration paid well in gold, ivory, slaves and souls. So satisfied was the Vatican with the progress made in the dual fields of commerce and religion that the Portuguese were granted by the Pope in his Bull of 8 January 1455, the monopoly of the trade with all the places they discovered on their expeditions provided that no war materials were traded with people and places not of the Roman Catholic faith. The mercantile clauses of the Bull granting this Papal monopoly set the general pattern for all trade monopolies subsequently granted by European countries to their own chartered national East India companies during the next three hundred years.

Henry the Navigator's death in 1460 removed the brains and the driving force that lay behind these striking exploration activities of Portugal, and in the next decade or so under Afonso V, Henry's nephew, they underwent a marked diminution. But with Afonso' death in 1481 and the succession of his son John II, the Portuguese crown re-entered the field of exploration with greater energy than ever. In 1482 John II placed Diogo Cão in charge of an expedition which, from 1482–1484, explored the mouth of the Congo River and Cape St. Augustine, and from 1485–1486, then explored as far south as Cape Cross and Cape Negro. But John II, like Henry the Navigator before him, was even more inspired by the religious significance of the discovery of new lands and new peoples than he was by their commercial value; and so, mindful of the Vatican's hope of making contact with Prester John, King John dispatched two expeditions, one by land and one by sea, to visit India and *en route* to search for this mysterious figure of the East. The former expedition was organized by Pedro de Covilhã and Affonso de Paiva, and in 1487 they reached India via Cairo and Aden. Later on their way back, they followed the east African coast as far south as the mouth of the Zambesi River without getting any information at all of either Prester John or the route round the Cape.

The other expedition was placed under the

command of Bartolomeu Dias and his instructions were that if he were able to discover a sea passage joining the Atlantic and the Indian Ocean to the south of the continent, he was to navigate it and then search up the African east coast as far as he could for evidence of Prester John's existence. The first part of his task was accomplished unknowingly, for from December 1487 to February 1488 he encountered almost continuous storms. When at last the weather cleared enough for him to determine his position and approach land with safety, he found himself sailing north-east along a hilly shore. He had obviously rounded the southern tip of the continent, but when he reached as far north as what are now known as Morsel Bay and the mouth of the Great Fish River, trouble with his crew forced him to abandon the second part of his mission — the search for Prester John. Retracing his steps, he redoubled the Cape and brought his ship safely back to Portugal, thereby earning the distinction for his country of being the first European to round the Cape.

During the next few years, Portugal was beset with internal troubles and with disputes with Spain; much of her programme of exploration had therefore to be curtailed, but the study of the findings of the earlier expeditions continued, and especially after the return of the Dias and Covilhã parties, the belief in the existence of a sea passage around the south of Africa became more and more commonly held, and the despatch of an expedition for the purpose of proving this and of reaching India by sea became more and more justified. To authorize such an expedition was one of the early decisions taken by Manuel I after he ascended the Portuguese throne in 1495.

VASCO DA GAMA (1469–1524)

THE HONOUR OF BEING APPOINTED to lead this expedition fell to Vasco da Gama, the son of the Comptroller of the Household of King Afonso. While full recognition must be given to the achievements of his many predecessors, including Dias, his success and the subsequent results of his epoch-making discoveries cause his achievement to rank first among those of all his compatriot maritime explorers.

Vasco da Gama sailed from the Tagus in command of a flotilla of four ships on 8 July 1497 and had an uneventful voyage until he rounded the Cape in the following November. Here, like Dias a decade before him, he encountered terrible storms and his success in the face of these difficulties was made immortal in the poem *Os Lusíadas* by Camoens who, when he was going to India as a soldier in the Portuguese army more than half a century later, followed Vasco da Gama's route round the Cape of Good Hope. Camoens had by then already started writing his epic and it was his experiences on his voyage to India that led him to make Vasco da Gama's historic voyage the central theme of his poem. His pen picture of the difficulties encountered by da Gama when rounding the Cape of Good Hope has led other artists to depict them also, each in his own medium. Two examples of these — one by a sculptor and the other by an artist — were to be seen in Macao, but now only the former of these remains. It is carved in low relief on a marble panel on the western face of the Vasco da Gama monument in the Vasco da Gama Gardens.

The other was a picture in blue and white tiles which until the 1970s graced a wall in the house of the late Dr P.J. Lobo on the Praia Grande. A photograph of it can be seen below.

16

The *Vasco da Gama* memorial in the gardens and avenue of the same name, at the foot of Guia Hill. On it is carved in relief, a scene from the epic poem 'Os Lusíadas' by Camoens, depicting Venus leading the Portuguese ships into the Indian Ocean despite fierce opposition from the monster Adamastor.

Azulejos of the monster Adamastor, formerly on the wall of Dr P.J. Lobo's house on the Praia Grande since demolished.

After rounding the Cape of Good Hope, Vasco da Gama led his ships north, visiting a number of East African ports on the way. He was in Quilimane in January 1498, Mozambique in March, and then continued north as far as Mombasa and Malindi. At this latter place, he stopped to take stock of the situation and from the information gathered concerning Indian Ocean trade, he decided to go straight to its centre — to Calicut on the Indian Malabar coast. This was a stroke of genius; many a lesser man would have searched the Indian Ocean for a port from which to challenge Calicut. Vasco da Gama, however, engaged an Arab captain as his pilot and sailed direct to Calicut where he immediately made a favourable impression on the authorities and established friendly relations with them. From this centre of oriental trade, he was able to observe how the merchandise from the Far East and from the Spice Isles, from the East Indies and Ceylon, was channelled at Calicut through Muslim hands across the Arabian Sea to the Persian Gulf or to the Red Sea, and thence overland to the Mediterranean. He also saw that by capturing this trade he would be both enriching Portugal and striking a blow for the Cross against the Crescent.

When he returned to Portugal with this information, he was able to report also that further east than India were wealthy countries peopled by races belonging to civilizations more ancient than any in the West. As evidence of their achievements, he took to his Queen gifts from 'The Land of the Chins': utensils and ornaments made of porcelain, a material hitherto unknown in the West.

In 1502, he made a second voyage to India, this time in command of a merchant fleet of 20 vessels, and on his third voyage, in 1524, he returned to India, as Viceroy of Goa. But as he died soon after his arrival, it is not as an administrator that Vasco da Gama is remembered, but as a great commander of voyages of discovery. When he originally arrived in India, he found two professions already well organized for dealing with oriental merchandise: the carrying trade and pirate trade. Regarding these, the Portuguese policy in the eastern seas at that time was to capture the trade and to subdue the piracy, and this was accomplished in the amazingly short time of a decade and a half, mainly due to the efforts and ability of two men — Dom Francisco de Almeida and Afonso de Albuquerque; but even these men and their companions could never have achieved this had it not been for the foundations so well laid by Vasco da Gama.

In estimating the importance to the world of this achievement, we are prone to recognize and consider only the effects that such achievement of the West had on the East. But to assess the true value of Portugal's overseas discoveries, we must also compute the reverse effect which the discovered

orient had on the occident, and this was just as phenomenal and far-reaching culturally, philosophically and theologically, as it was in mercantile and political affairs. The main Christian countries of the West found they had to reorientate — in more senses of the word than one — their thinking when they 'discovered' civilizations with treasures of art, music, literature, philosophy and civil codes of behaviour, not based on Christian principles, and yet comparable with those of the west. Macao, and Hong Kong later, played a significant part in this opening of the occidental mind to the civilizations of the East. For two centuries or more, Macao was the only avenue of approach to China's learning that was open to Westerners and, unlike Marco Polo who arrived by an overland route some centuries earlier, most of those using Macao were missionaries. But like Marco Polo, many of them also used their writings to introduce and interpret the East to the West. Of the missionaries, first came the Portuguese under their *padroado*, then the Jesuits of many nationalities, Italian, French, Belgian and German as well as Portuguese. Of these, the greatest was undoubtedly Matteo Ricci, an Italian Jesuit, who after some years in Goa and Cochin, arrived in Macao in 1582 with the intention of entering China. In this he was finally successful and after working long years in Shiu Hing, Nanchang and Nanking, he eventually reached Peking in 1601. By the time of his death in 1610 he had compiled and sent back to Europe what remains to this day a standard work on Chinese life, institutions and philosophy. More than two centuries after the arrival of the Roman Catholics came the Protestants, and they also used Macao as their China base. First came Robert Morrison (and later his son J.R. Morrison, not a missionary), then Milne, Medhurst (and also James Legge in Hong

Kong), all from Britain. Gutzlaff came from the continent of Europe, and Parker, Wells-Williams and Speer from America, and all wrote to ensure that the treasures of Chinese thought and philosophy might become more readily available to the scholars of the West.

In European mercantile and political spheres, the initial Portuguese contacts with the East resulted in shifts of trade and power centres from the eastern Mediterranean, Levantine and mid-European states to the cities of the Atlantic seaboard. Lisbon, and later Antwerp, Amsterdam and London, all became world market centres and remained so for centuries. The coming of cottons and cheaper silks changed habits and fashions in dress throughout western Europe while the introduction of spices and new fruits, plants and vegetables revolutionized cuisine, diets and pharmacopoeias. The trade rivalries they engendered led to the rise of many Western nations — Spain, Portugal, Netherlands, France, Britain and the United States of America — and in their turn, to the fall of most of them as imperial world powers. Each strove for world supremacy in trade through supremacy at sea, and through the acquisition of the territories whose trade they had captured. All this worldwide change arose as the direct result of the link between Europe and India forged by Vasco da Gama at the end of the fifteenth century, and made his discovery of the sea route to India one of the greatest historical events that occurred between the beginning of the Christian era and the onset of the modern age of science. The Spanish historian Gomara was blessed with prophetic sight when in 1553 he described the Spanish and Portuguese discovery of the ocean routes to the East and West Indies as 'the greatest event since the creation of the world, apart from the incarnation and death of him [sic] who created it'.

At the time of Gomara's writing, the full impact of the Iberian discoveries had hardly even begun to effect the rest of Europe, but now we know that it was the rounding of the Cape of Good Hope, together with that of The Horn and the circumnavigation of the earth, that made it possible to contemplate the human race as essentially one, and the eastern and western ends of the earth as coincidental points.

Macao's recognition of Vasco da Gama's major role in the discoveries leading to its own settlement was expressed by its citizens when they named an avenue and one of their public gardens after him, and in the latter, erected to his memory a stone monument surmounted by his bust in bronze.

ALMEIDA AND ALBUQUERQUE

PORTUGUESE POLICY EAST of the Cape was, in the early stages, decided by King Manuel himself and its execution was entrusted to the leaders of missions sent out from time to time to implement specific portions of this policy. But during the first decade of the sixteenth century an overall policy began to emerge which called for implementation by an official resident in the area over a longer period than just one voyage. When the post was established the appointee was variously called Viceroy, or Governor, or Captain-General or Governor-General, of Portuguese India, but later, when Goa became the centre of Portuguese activity in the East, he was generally known as the Viceroy of Goa. The first appointment was made in 1505 when Dom Francisco de Almeida became Viceroy; his immediate task was to wrest from the Moorish control, the oriental trade to Europe which was using the Red Sea and the Persian Gulf routes to

The bronze bust of Vasco da Gama on his Macao monument.

the eastern Mediterranean. He sailed from Lisbon with a fleet of twenty-two ships on 25 March of that year to assume his duties. Almeida's main contributions to the Portuguese cause were the founding of a number of trading settlements on the African and west Indian coasts and his victory over the Moslem fleet at Diu in 1509. However, he did not realize the importance of fortifying these bases, nor did he appreciate the efforts of those who did. This particularly applied to Afonso de Albuquerque who, in spite of his difficulties with Almeida, later became the architect of Portugal's maritime empire in the orient.

When Afonso de Albuquerque left Lisbon on 18 April 1506 as Chief Captain of six ships, he carried with him a letter from King Manuel appointing him as Almeida's successor as from 1508, the end of the latter's three-year appointment. This situation, plus the fact that the two men did not see eye to eye on plans or policy, inevitably led to friction between them, and it in turn gave rise to the atmosphere that conspirators thrive in. At the end of his term of office, Almeida refused to hand over to Albuquerque and it was not until 1509 that the latter became Governor. While waiting, Albuquerque had time to review the situation and his conclusion was that Portugal needed not only a portion of Asia's trade with Europe, but its complete control. Only by this means could the Moslem enemies of Christendom be subdued. To accomplish this Portugal needed fortified bases, not just trading bases, at strategic points throughout the African,

Indian and Arabian coasts of the Indian Ocean. These Albuquerque set up and operating from them, he freed the Arabian Sea of major threats from both pirates and Moors, and, when Goa was captured and fortified in 1511, it became Golden Goa, the centre of this new empire. Albuquerque then turned his attention to what we now know as the Far East.

In the eastern region of the Indian Ocean — often then referred to as Further India — Portugal ultimately adopted a policy similar to that pursued by them in the Arabian Sea. Briefly, it was to establish their control over the China and Spice Islands trade operating from a base such as Malacca. The first move to implement this policy was made in 1508 when Diogo Lopes de Sequeira was commissioned by King Manuel to proceed to the island of S. Lourenço (Madagascar) in search of spices — especially cloves — which Tristão da Cunha had reported grew there in abundance. If these and medicinal plants were not available there, he was to continue on to Malacca. Here he was to investigate the spice trade and was specifically instructed to follow up Vasco da Gama's report and to seek full information concerning 'the Chijns', their country, their merchandise and their religion. Diogo Lopes did not find his visit to S. Lourenço very rewarding so he sailed with his four ships for Malacca, arriving there on 11 September 1509. He informed the King of Malacca that he had come to trade and, if possible, to negotiate a trade treaty, and these proposals were so favourably entertained that the Portuguese were given permission to land and to begin trading. The King also made some houses near the shore available to them for use as a factory, but this generous treatment soon aroused the jealousy of the Moors who warned the King that these apparently peaceful merchants were really there to capture his city and enslave his people. The Moors were successful in arousing the King's suspicion and he planned to capture and massacre all the Portuguese. When his plans were almost completed, a Malayan woman, friendly with one of the Portuguese, warned them of their danger, and enabled the ships to escape although all the factory staff were overpowered after a stubborn resistance, and were taken prisoners. After making unsuccessful attempts to rescue them, Diogo Lopes and his ships sailed for Colombo whence he himself eventually returned safely to Lisbon, arriving there in 1510. He gave a glowing account to King Manuel of the riches of Malacca, but apart from reporting having seen a few Chinese junks in its harbour, he brought back no information concerning China or its trade.

In spite of this setback, Malacca remained the keystone of the Portuguese plans for their trade expansion in Further India. It lay athwart the routes to the East Indies in the south and to China and Japan in the north, and so Albuquerque in Goa decided to take a hand in retrieving the situation himself. With this object in view he arrived in Malacca on 1 July 1511. His first task to effect the liberation of those of Diogo Lopes's men who were still alive in Malacca prisons, but, when it became evident to him that he was not going to achieve the release of his compatriots by negotiations only, he resorted to force. On 15 August 1511 he captured the town and added it to his country's growing list of eastern fortresses. By chance, some Chinese traders were in Malacca at the time, and Albuquerque's action won their admiration and support to such an extent that they assisted him in sending a trade envoy to Siam. Siam was chosen by Albuquerque as his first step to China because it had direct trade and political associations with Malacca, the King of Siam having been largely responsible for its establishment as a port early in the fifteenth century.

The success of this mission to Siam convinced Albuquerque of the trade potential of that part of Asia which appealed to him all the more when he found it was not, like Malacca, an area dominated by Moslems. So, after firmly establishing his administration in Malacca, he began to plan further expeditions to other parts of the Far East, reserving for himself the command of a mission to the land of his newly found friends — China. But the completion of his China plan was to fall to the lot of another. First he had to return to India where he found that his long absence at Malacca had given some of his rivals the opportunity of continuing their conspiracy against him. Immediately on arrival he dealt decisively with this situation and then proceeded to complete the first part of his Arabian Sea plans by capturing Ormuz. The next phase of these plans included the capture of Aden, but the preparations for this operation had to be made in India. He therefore sailed for Goa, but while en route, when near Muscat, he received a dispatch from Lisbon informing him of his replacement as Governor of Goa. Where all his enemies throughout the orient had failed, a few conspirators at the Lisbon court had succeeded. 'In bad repute with men because of the King, and in bad repute with the King because of men. It were well that I were gone' was his comment, and apparently his resolve. The rest of his trip to Goa he spent putting his personal, his official and his spiritual affairs in order, and, after spending the night of 15 December 1515 at anchor outside Goa near the bar, he did not live to cross it, but instead crossed life's bar, brokenhearted, an hour before the next sunrise.

Albuquerque's success in setting up Portugal's overseas empire was due to his strong and endearing personality and to his talents for administration, displayed in both peace and war. Although he has no stone memorial of his own in Macao, spiritually he shares that of Vasco da Gama which no one could look upon without also being reminded of Almeida and Albuquerque, and those others of da Gama's immediate successors, without whom there could not have been a Portuguese Macao. In recognition of this, one of Macao's streets proudly carries the name: *Rua de Afonso de Albuquerque.*

Street sign bearing the name of Afonso de Albuquerque.

JORGE ÁLVARES

MACAO'S PUBLIC MONUMENT to Jorge Álvares is the work of a leading Portuguese sculptor, Euclides Vaz. It stands at the junction of Avenida Dr Mário Soares and Avenida da Praia Grande, facing the Government Departments Building. That statue was unveiled on 16 September 1954. On 3 December 1966, during the disturbances that convulsed Macao, the statue was attacked and damaged by rampaging youths. Following the restoration of public order to Macao, the statue was repaired. It is still in place, though now overlooks the new reclamation, unlike, as formerly, the beautiful curve of the Praia Grande.

Both its artistic composition and its orientation are historically significant, and these, combined with the achievements of Alvares himself, make it the most locally important of all Macao's monuments. Nevertheless, it owes its presence here to a misunderstanding, to be described in more detail later.

Álvares had his first introduction to the Far East when, as a junior officer with Albuquerque, he arrived in Malacca in 1511. It is not known whether he took part in the mission which Albuquerque sent to Siam, but it is evident that he quickly rose in the esteem of his senior officers because when the first Governor of Malacca decided to carry on with Albuquerque's plan of sending a mission to China, Alvares was appointed to its command. His amicable dealings with the Chinese were subsequently to prove the wisdom of placing Álvares in charge of this first official visit of the Portuguese to China.

He sailed from Malacca in May 1513 and his China landfall was at an island in the Pearl River estuary known in English as Lintin and in Cantonese as Ling Ting (伶仃), meaning 'Solitary Nail'. This island had long been known by the Portuguese and the Malays by various names, meaning in their respective languages, the Island of Trade, in addition to which it was the only port in south China at that time where the mandarins were known to connive at foreign trade. The anchorage between the island and Nam Tau (藍頭) on the mainland was called by the Cantonese Tuen Mun (屯門), while to the Portuguese it was known as Tamão or Ta-meng. (Map 1) Álvares commemorated the completion of his outward journey — as was the custom of Portuguese explorers — by erecting a 'King's mark' or *padrão* at the site of his landing on the island. This token also marked life's journey's end for Alvares's young son who was accompanying him. He died while the mission was on the island and he was buried at the foot of his father's *padrão*. Eight years later, the same *padrão* was used to mark the father's own final resting-place.

At the end of his first mission in April or May 1514, Álvares left Lintin with a valuable cargo of merchandise for Malacca where the success of his expedition was immediately recognized. In some ways, this proved to be unfortunate as it provoked a number of visits of Portuguese ships to China, some under less disciplined control than others, and many attempting to use other ports along the coast than those recognized unofficially by the Chinese as possible trading posts.

For two or three years after his return to Malacca, Álvares seems to have been engaged exclusively on local administrative affairs; but his personal knowledge of China, its customs and its people was soon again in official demand. In 1517 he sailed with Fernão Peres de Andrade whose squadron was given the assignment of taking as far as Canton, Portugal's first envoy to China, Tome Pires. The fleet called at the Tuen Mun anchorage off Lintin

The monument to Jorge Álvares, standing on Macao's Outer Harbour reclamation as it appeared after the riots of 1–2–3 December 1966.

and that of his men led the Chinese to place credence in the rumours they had heard of the 'ferocious and predatory' way the Portuguese had treated the Moors and the Malays in Malacca. When therefore, Fernão Peres de Andrade left China to return to Malacca, he and his men left behind them such a bad reputation with the Chinese officials and with the people of Canton that it took the Portuguese many years to repair the damage done to the good relations already set up with the Chinese by Alvares during his first visit. But worse was to follow. It was reported to Peking that Andrade himself had assaulted a mandarin official at Lintin and this, on top of the other rumours resulted in a complete change of relations between the Portuguese and the Chinese. The mission of Tomé Pires was evicted from Peking before negotiations were concluded, and on arrival back in Canton in September 1521, all the members of the embassy were imprisoned and those who were not executed forthwith, ultimately died there as prisoners.

Fortunately Álvares arrived back safely in Malacca just in time to distinguish himself in another sphere of service — the defence of the city against the Malays. But it was not long before his experience was required again in China, and this time he was in charge of the mission, which arrived at Lintin early in 1521. Yet, but before he had time to repair the damaged relations with China, his visit ended tragically with his death in Lintin on 8 July of that year. He was buried near the *padrão* which he himself had erected eight years earlier.

Jorge Álvares never, at any time as far as we know, set foot on the Macao peninsula itself, but it was his work in the area that made Macao's subsequent foundation possible. His record of discovery, and his powers of fostering good relations between different peoples, merit the position his

and then, when all the entry formalities had been completed, it proceeded up river where Tome Pires disembarked. Álvares then returned to Malacca with the fleet, arriving there in September 1518, but this time he remained for a short period only. In 1519 he was again en route to China, but now as an officer in Simão Peres de Andrade's unfortunate mission, unfortunate because Andrade's behaviour monument has been given in the city that was built on the foundations of his early labours. It also explains why he is depicted in his memorial with a replica of his *padrão* at his back and his right arm upraised in the direction of his first China landing and his last resting place, a mere twenty-five miles away in distance but now four hundred and fifty years away in time.

The setting up of this Álvares monument, however, did not signify the end of his participation in the making of Macao's history. In December 1966, the riots which shook Macao almost to its foundations, began at this monument. The picture above shows that in his tussle with those who 'vapour and fume and brag', he lost merely his right forearm and hand, his nose and the toes of his left foot. But his page in Macao's history is indelible and indestructible, thanks to the camera and the printing press, and all the rioters achieved was to draw further attention to his achievements by passing into the class with the other one-armed Macao history makers: Ferreira do Amaral and Antonio de Albuquerque de Coelho.

SIXTEENTH CENTURY SINO-PORTUGUESE-JAPANESE RELATIONS

THE STORY OF the dealings between the Chinese and the Portuguese during the next thirty years is not a happy one. The piratical behaviour of Simão de Andrade resulted in a complete change of Chinese relations, and in addition to the action taken by the Chinese as already outlined, all dealings with Portuguese 'adventurers' were henceforth officially forbidden by Peking, and further Portuguese

attempts to reopen trade with China were, for some time to come, resisted by force. Eventually, however, sporadic trading attempts (still officially illegal according to Peking, but treated with a blind eye and an open palm as far as the local mandarins were concerned) were made at various places along the Kwangtung, Fukien and Chekiang coasts. At two such places off the Kwangtung coast, these attempts achieved a definite measure of success and they ultimately assumed considerable importance in the future development of Macao. They were the islands of Sheung Chuen (上川) and Lampacao (浪白澳). These trade attempts were mainly small separate ventures based on Malacca, and were made by junks which sailed along the China seaboard in search of a chance to trade. The trade breakthrough eventually came in an unexpected way through Japan.

One of these Portuguese junks from Malacca happened to sail much further north than usual (whether purposely, or due solely to bad weather is hard to say), and was wrecked on a Japanese island during a gale. The stranded Portuguese were well treated ashore and were quick to take advantage of this chance contact by establishing as friendly relations as possible with all the Japanese, both official and private, whom they met. The members of the shipwrecked crew eventually returned safely to Malacca and since Japan had not yet closed its doors to foreign trade, the Portuguese followed up this chance contact with other trading visits. These private efforts proved successful, and the Portuguese officials regularized this advance in their prospect of trade with Japan by replacing the haphazard ventures with a monopoly system that they had already found to work successfully in the development of their trade in the Indian ocean, the Arabian Sea and the Persian Gulf.

The essential feature of this system was that the monopoly of all Portugal's trade in any one area was vested in one man, generally as a reward for his services to his sovereign. The appointment was made annually and carried with it two distinct responsibilities, a personal mercantile one, and an official civil one. The former gave him the opportunity to make or recoup his fortune, while the latter gave him the official status and authority without which the former could not really be successful. In this Pacific region, the title of the appointment was Capitão-Mor (Captain-Major of the Voyage of China and Japan), and the civil responsibility of the holder extended beyond the personnel on board the ship or ships under his command, to all Portuguese citizens in temporary or permanent settlements ashore in his area, and this responsibility included being the official Portuguese representative to the nearby foreign countries, in this case, especially to China and Japan. If, as sometimes happened, the voyage was not completed within twelve months owing to unfavourable weather or trading conditions, the appointment continued until the voyage terminated; in such cases it might well happen that two or more appointments overlapped in any one area and then seniority in the settlement in that area was determined solely by the date of the commission from the King, or from the Viceroy of Goa in his name. Continuous records exist concerning the holders of this post in the China seas from 1550 to 1640, and to Professor Boxer we are indebted for a clear exposition of the contribution made by these men to Macao's early development.

The voyage from Malacca was a long one in both time and distance, and the route traversed the transitional belt between the regions of the north-east and the south-west monsoons. In the days of sail, this transition area was often the scene of a long hold-up awaiting favourable winds, but if by any chance water and food supplies or anchorages where ships could be careened or repaired were also available there, the enforced stop-over was turned to some advantage. On the route between Malacca and Japan, this transition area is situated along the Kwangtung coast, which is also about the mid-point of the journey. The Portuguese were therefore forced to seek the use of suitable offshore islands in the area where their presence could more easily go unofficially unnoticed or conveniently ignored by the local mandarins, than if they landed on the mainland. The islands of Sheung Chuen and Lampacao just referred to were two such islands.

ST. JOHN'S ISLAND, LAMPACAO AND AH-MA-KAO

ST. JOHN'S, ECHOING the Cantonese name for the island, is what the first English seafaring visitors to the island of Sheung Chuen (上川) called it. It is also variously called Shang Chuen, Shan Chuan, San Chun, or San Chuang, sometimes written as one word, sometimes as two. It is situated just off the China coast about 60 miles south-west of Macao, and was frequently used by the Portuguese trading ships as a temporary matshed stopping-place on their way to and from Japan during the trading season of August to November of the years around 1550. One of its claims to a place in history is that Francis Xavier, 'The Apostle of the Orient', after introducing Christianity to Japan, died on the island in 1552 while waiting for permission to enter China. Although his remains were removed the following year to Malacca, the island continued as a place of Christian pilgrimage until China was again closed to foreigners in recent years.

St. John's Island, in spite of its use in the trading season, was not a very safe anchorage during a strong monsoon or a typhoon for either the unwieldy Portuguese carrack or não or even for the large junk so universally used on the China coast. For this reason this island was abandoned about 1554–1555 as an annual place of call in favour of Lampacao, 20 miles nearer the mouth of the Canton or Pearl River; this island, originally called Lam-pac-kao by the Portuguese, was known to the Cantonese as Long Pak Kong (浪白江). However, it was not found to be a completely satisfactory stopping-place either, for its anchorages were shallow and increasingly so due to the continuous silt deposits from the neighbouring Pearl River estuary; as it is but a step from Lam-pac-kao to Ah-ma-kao, it is not surprising that within a very short time the Portuguese were frequenting the latter anchorage in preference to the former.

There are various accounts of the actual circumstances which led to the change from the unsatisfactory international situation in the early 1520s, to the amicable one in 1557 when the Chinese transferred Ah-Ma-Kao and the surrounding peninsula to the Portuguese. The most commonly accepted version of the reason for this transfer is that the poor economic conditions prevailing in the area at the time had forced larger numbers than usual of the inhabitants of the coastal area to turn to piracy for a living, and that Ah-Ma-Kao had become the headquarters of a pirate band too strong for the local Chinese authorities to subdue or even to control. When much of the river and sea trade between Canton and its provincial coastal

ports became thus endangered, the mandarins appealed for help to the Captain-Major at Lampacao whose armed vessels were believed to be more than a match for the pirate junks.

No precise information appears to exist concerning the negotiations carried out between the mandarins and the Captain-Major, nor does there seem to be any authentic record in existence of the armed action subsequently taken against the pirates, but this one thing is certain that when this coastal area was finally freed of its scourge, Ah-ma-kao had become the first permanent and internationally recognized European foothold in China. While the exact conditions of the agreement may be a matter of dispute among twentieth-century politicians and historians, there can be no doubt that it was accepted as being true and binding at that time by the local official representatives of both the Emperor of China and the King of Portugal.

The advantages to the Portuguese of having a permanent and fixed settlement on the Kwangtung coast instead of a temporary and movable one is obvious, even if it was not a recognized port for Chinese trade. Ah-ma-kao had better deep-sea port facilities, better shelter for its shipping from both the south-west and north-east monsoon and at the same time providing a reasonably safe anchorage during typhoons. Having easy river access to Canton and its international and coastal trade routes, Ah-ma-kao was ideally situated to participate in this trade if ever China relaxed her rigid veto, and this is exactly what happened.

As Portuguese ships began to call regularly on their way back to Malacca laden with merchandise that was denied to the Chinese only because Japan closed her doors to trade with China, it was but a matter of time when it was realized that Ah-ma-kao was not China and that there was no Japanese impediment to China buying Japanese goods from the Portuguese, if they wished to have them. China needed silver, and Japan at that time wanted silk, so China only had to release her silk to the Portuguese and she was paid in silver, while Japan obtained what she wanted through one easily controlled channel without having to open up her country to trade from all China's ports. This trade triangle was doubly valuable to the Portuguese because the Chinese silk they sold in Japan paid handsomely for itself as well as for the Japanese merchandise bought there; they also commanded good prices in the markets of Malacca, India and Europe. Their Japanese trade was thus not undertaken by the Portuguese to the detriment of their own trade but as a supplement to it. It was also beneficial to the Chinese since it provided them with an outlet for their merchandise and at the same time was a source of the silver they so much needed; it freed them from the pirate threat to their trade and their sovereignty — a threat which they were incapable of dealing with themselves — and the permanent occupation of Ah-ma-kao by the Portuguese ensured against the return of the pirates to power in the area. Agreeing that Portugal could occupy Macao was far from being an unequal treaty for China; rather was the resulting Japanese trade an unforeseen bonus to her and a continuing one as long as Ah-ma-kao was not Chinese, and as long as Japan's prohibition of trade with China remained. It also proved to be of great long-term value to Macao because when rival European maritime powers later cut her lifeline to India and Europe, it was this trade plus the regional trade that developed along with it, which ensured her survival as a foreign port through to the early nineteenth century, when other saving factors began to operate. But before considering that later aspect of Macao's story, we turn back to sixteenth-century Ah-ma-kao and consider what effects this heightened opportunity for mutual prosperity, and a more friendly atmosphere for international relations, had on the development of this young settlement.

Portuguese Ah-Ma-Kao

ONE OF THE FIRST decisions necessitated by the change in status of Ah-ma-kao concerned an official Portuguese name for their newly acquired territory; the choice made was *Povoação do Nome de Deus na China* — The Settlement of the Name of God in China. This formal and documentary name being too cumbersome for general use, the most obvious European short title to adopt was one based on the Romanization Ah-ma-kao; the hyphens and vocal prefix 'Ah' (only needed in a monosyllabic language such as Chinese) were dropped and the 'k' displaced by the hard Portuguese 'c', resulting in Macao, the name by which this Portuguese possession has been generally known to Europeans from 1557 to the present day. This occidental name, however, is not used in either Chinese writing or conversation; locally Macao is called O-Moon, the Cantonese pronunciation of '澳門' meaning 'Shelter or Cove Gateway'.

The next decision that faced the Portuguese settlers of Ah-ma-kao concerned the physical problem of building their city. Fortunately, they wisely avoided the temptation to try and make it a Lisbon of the East, for its setting was the very antithesis of anything its new rulers had known in Europe. It was separated from their home country by the vast expanse of the Eurasian landmass or by months of hazardous journeying under sail via the Atlantic and Indian Oceans and the South China Sea; it lay on the edge of the eastern seaboard of Asia, where the compensations for its isolation and unfamiliar surroundings were found in the fruits of trade and of its religious zest, and in the permanent city built to replace the matsheds that characterized the temporary shelters on the beaches of Sheung Chuen and Lampacao islands. It was inevitable that the residences, churches, hospitals, business houses, roads, forts and port facilities thus needed — in fact all the communal necessities of this Portuguese sixteenth-century overseas settlement — should bear the Iberian stamp. It was this as well as its new form of government that differentiated Portuguese Macao so much from Chinese Ah-ma-kao, and added just that touch of Mediterranean charm that still distinguishes Macao from the other cities of the China coast.

CITY OF MACAO AND ITS SENATE

WE HAVE ALREADY noted that the Church was always well to the fore in any move made by Portugal's merchant adventurers, and that the trade settlements which were set up along their sea-lanes soon became beads of bishoprics on an orient-encircling rosary as well. This close association of church and state enabled the former to exercise its guidance — and where it thought necessary, its control — over the political and trade changes contemplated by the latter. An example of this guidance is the way in which the church helped Macao to make its first move towards setting up a democratic form of local government.

In 1585, the Bishop of the Diocese of Macao took the democratic and progressive step of calling a meeting of the leading Portuguese citizens to consider the establishment of a local municipal council. Since its founding almost thirty years previously, the settlement had not received any formal recognition from either Lisbon or Peking and it had thus far operated solely under the mutual recognition that existed between the senior local Portuguese official, that is, the Captain-Major of the Voyage of China and Japan, and the senior Chinese mandarin in the neighbouring part of the Kwangtung province. But with the almost complete abandonment of Lam-pac-kao in favour of Macao, a more responsible form of local government was needed in the latter to cope with the rapid increase in population and trade which its foundation promoted. It may well be that this public venture of a bishop beyond his ecclesiastical confines into the realms of democratic politics was not altogether unrelated to the change in royal allegiance to Philip II of Spain which the Portuguese nation had recently been compelled to accept. These Iberian events

may also account for the unusual political unanimity shown by the Macao community when they adopted the Bishop's recommendation at a public meeting and forthwith set up a local council. Ultimately this action received official approval — and the new council its official recognition — when the Viceroy of Goa, on 10 April 1586, authorized Macao to assume that measure of local self-government which was usually enjoyed by Portugal's home cities of similar size and standing. It was later granted the same status and privileges as the city of Évora in Portugal, and Macao's official name was changed from 'Settlement' to 'City', from *Povoação* to *Cidade do Nome de Deus na China*.

The Senate — *Senado* — which the Macao people set up must have been one of the most democratic forms of government then known. It was composed of three elected Aldermen (*Vereadores*) and three appointed officials together with a secretary, and was unique in that it had no long-term chairman. The duties of that post rotated among the elected members, a new appointment being made each month. Another of its members was appointed annually to be responsible to the Senate for all the Chinese affairs of the colony, both internal and external. He was the *Procurador da Cidade* (Municipal Attorney), and all communications from Chinese officials were directed, in the first instance, to him and not to either the Captain-Major or to the Chairman of the Senate. The Chinese subsequently made him a junior mandarin and thereafter always accorded him the privileges and precedence enjoyed by an official of that rank, and continued to do so even after 1623 when a Portuguese Governor was appointed in Macao.

The powers and duties of the Senate which were taken over in 1586 from the Captain-Major may be briefly described as being the administration of the whole of the civil affairs of the colony. Special provision was made in the Royal Decree of 16 February 1586 for transferring the responsibility for judicial affairs from the Captain-Major to the Senate, and it discharged this added duty through a Magistrate *(Ouvidor)* who was appointed for a year or at the most two years at a time. This became a doubly important post, for if the young city was ever left without a Captain-Major — and this could frequently happen since the demands of his shipboard duties took precedence over those of his constituency ashore — the *Ouvidor* and a *Capitão da Terra* elected by the Senate shared the gubernatorial duties of the absent Captain-Major.

There was only one public body which was senior to the Senate. It was the General Council *(Conselho Geral)*, and it met only on rare and special occasions. It consisted of the leading ecclesiastical authorities and private citizens, together with the senior military officers, all sitting in council with the Senate. A similar system of government was in operation in other Portuguese colonies, but in none of these did the Senate take such a responsible part in the affairs of its community as it did in Macao. Here there was no Inquisition, the Portuguese church dignitaries were mostly liberal patriots and the Captain-Major's local powers were rigidly held in check by the Senate. So jealously did this body guard its democratic powers that the Captain-Major's command in the colony was confined to the defences and to the garrison. Nevertheless, although he was only indirectly responsible to the King through his immediate superior, the Viceroy of Goa, he was recognized as the senior official in the colony and his appointment was always ultimately approved by the King personally. This relationship of the Senate to the Captain-Major remained even

when the appointment of the latter was upgraded in 1623 to that of Governor and Captain-General, and its duration increased to a period of three years, fully resident in the colony.

This democratic form of government lasted until the establishment of the Liberal Constitutional Monarchy in Portugal in 1783 when the Senate's powers were reduced to those of a mere municipal council.

The Senate was accommodated in its own building *(Senado da Câmara)* which stood on the Largo do Senado, facing the central city square where its successor now stands; even though it is not the original Senado da Câmara, the present building is so intimately associated with many of Macao's historic events that it is now a monument in its own right, as well as being the seat of the city's local governing body. Indeed the very name *Leal Senado* (Loyal Senate), which the present building proudly and justly bears, is conspicuous evidence that it stands for the glories of the past as well as for the needs and duties of the present.

In both its recent and in its more distant past, the Senate has experienced more than its fair share of uneasy days. As relatively recently as December 1966, the building and its contents suffered more in two days at the hands of rioters 'who break through and steal' than they did throughout two centuries of exposure to the corruption of 'moth and rust'. Fortunately, no serious structural damage was sustained by the building but many of its files of irreplaceable records were destroyed together with historic pictures and period furniture.

A little over a century ago, the building was the site of a regrettable incident in which an armed party from a British man-of-war forcibly set free a British Hong Kong resident who was being temporarily detained there in custody. This fortunately is the only occasion in which the building itself has suffered foreign armed interference. It avoided such subjection even during Portugal's 60 years under Spanish rule (1580–1640) and also during the period when Japan overran South East Asia in World War II (1941–1945). The Senate's earlier difficulties were mainly all constitutional teething troubles, the most serious of them being due to the friction that developed between the Captain-Major or the Governor and the Senate before the colony had attained an even administrative keel. Many of the early reports to Goa and to Lisbon, which were so derogatory to the Senate and the reverse of flattering to Macao itself, arose directly out of this friction because very early in its existence (probably due to its sound initial launching by Bishop Leonardo de Sá and also due to the advantages the resident councillors had over the bird-of-passage Captains-Major) the Senate established itself as the real governing body of Macao. Is it any wonder that the Captains-Major were dissatisfied with their minor lot and that Lisbon could not gather a clear picture of Macao from the biased reports they were receiving from them? In 1635, the Senate decided to ensure that Lisbon was aware of the true facts as they saw them concerning Macao; they therefore sent a memorial to the Crown setting forth the accomplishments of the Senate; its argument may be summarized in this extract:

> This city of the Name of God, situated in this Kingdom of Great China, has grown from humble beginnings to be one of the greatest that Your Majesty has in the State of India. And it has survived hitherto solely because of its trade and commerce, being maintained and developed at the cost of its citizens with lavish disbursements of their wealth, both in heavily bribing the Chinese, as in building walls and fortifications, something quite unprecedented in China, founding cannon, constructing a powder magazine, and providing the necessary munitions and war material for its defence.

As well as drawing the attention of Lisbon to Macao's achievements of self-reliance and self-support during her first hundred years, it made Lisbon aware of Macao's loyalty to her during the sixty years of submission to Spanish rule. Following Portugal's emancipation, there came a change regarding Macao. In 1654, the Governor and Captain-General, João de Sousa Pereira, 'in the name of the King our Lord, Dom João IV', ordered an inscription to be cut in stone as a 'testimony of the exceeding loyalty of its [Macao's] inhabitants'. The inscription proclaimed: 'City of the Name of God. There is none more loyal.' That this message was placed over the stairway in the senate building has often been taken to imply that it refers specifically to the Senate. This is an error for the inscription clearly states that it refers to Macao's 'inhabitants' as a whole. The loyalty of the Senate did not become a matter for public recognition until the official title of Leal Senado was conferred on the municipal council [of Macao] by the Prince Regent of Portugal from his refuge at Rio de Janeiro in 1810, the Camara having previously used the prefix 'Nobre' [Noble] as did that of Goa. Supporting details concerning the circumstances under which the title was granted are also given by Father Teixeira. On 20 February 1809, the Senate decided to send a loyal memorial to Prince John in Brazil, congratulating him on safely establishing his regency there after being forced to flee from Lisbon when Napoleon embarked on his plan of partitioning Portugal. The Senate took advantage of this opportunity of direct contact with Prince John to acquaint him personally with conditions in the Far East and of the accomplishments of his subjects in Macao. In their memorial members of the Senate referred, *inter alia*, to the frequent financial aid sent to Goa by Macao and acquainted the Regent of their successful operations against the notorious pirate bands that had been on the increase in that region throughout the decade. These had become a serious threat to all trade using the island-studded seas east of Macao, the Kwangtung coast and islands as far west as Hainan Island and even high up the Canton River above the estuary limits, almost threatening Whampoa. The leader of these pirate bands at the time was the notorious Kam Pau Sai, alias Apotsi (Ah-po-tsai) and it was the operations planned by the *Dezembargador* (Chief Judge) and Master of Customs — Senhor Miguel de Arriaga Brum de Silveira — that enabled Macao to repeat its successes of 1557 and rid its neighbourhood of this pirate scourge. It was on the basis of the reports of these achievements that the Regent, on 13 May 1810, conferred the title '*Leal*' on Macao's Senate.

Again in 1818, the Leal Senado, as it was by then known, had further direct associations with Prince John. The occasion this time was the celebrations held in honour of his accession to the throne of Portugal as King John VI. The Leal Senado chose as their delegate to represent Macao at Rio de Janeiro on 6 February 1818, **Domingos Pio Marques**, the son of Domingos Marques. Domingos Pio Marques was born in Macao on 6 May 1783 and there he married Inacia Francisca Baptista Cortela on 21 November 1803. While in Brazil, Pio Marques was able to assure the new King personally of the continued loyalty of Macao of a measure no less than that which he had enjoyed

from the colony during his long Regency. When Marques arrived back in Macao on 14 October 1818, he brought with him a letter of appreciation from the King to the Senate and to the people of Macao, thanking them for their past loyalty and for the promise of its continuation in the future.

In the light therefore of this evidence there can no longer be any doubt that the title 'Leal Senado' was not bestowed — as has been generally believed until recently — because of the refusal of the Senate to acknowledge allegiance to Spain or to fly the Spanish flag during the period of submission. Regarding these two points, it must be noted that although in Macao acknowledgment of Portugal's submission to Spain was delayed for several months, the Captain-Major, two Bishops, the Jesuit Rector, the Senate members and leading citizens did eventually take the oath of allegiance to Philip II of Spain on 18 December 1582. Furthermore, Professor Boxer has pointed out that by flying the Portuguese flag throughout the period of submission, Macao was merely acting in accordance with the terms of the agreement of the Cortes of Thomar of 1581 by which **all** Portuguese colonies were to continue using their old national flag and their own administrative procedures, King Philip II of Spain having pledged himself to rule all his acquired Portuguese lands as King Philip I of Portugal, and not as the King of Spain. The title *Leal* was thus bestowed on the Senado in 1810, not because of its record during the period 1580 to 1640, but because it was the most fitting way in which Portugal could acknowledge the unswerving loyalty to her of the whole of Macao's people during the first two and a half centuries of the colony's existence.

During this long period, Macao was the only one of Portugal's overseas possessions which has not contributed a single individual to any of the so-called independence movements which exist, on however small a scale, in all the others. That statement is as true today as it was when it was first made.

In this connection, and in fairness to the Macao Portuguese, it should be noted that the local Chinese were not then included in the terms 'the Macao people' or 'its inhabitants'. In the very early days of the settlement, the Chinese were permitted to stay in Macao during daylight only; at nightfall they returned to their homes in nearby villages and the city gates were shut until the next morning. As this safety precaution was, in the course of time, gradually relaxed, the Chinese came to live in Macao in increasing numbers and thus the mandarins, retaining their interest in their nationals, were gradually able later to re-establish their interest and influence in the settlement itself too. The loyalty of most of the Chinese in Macao in these early days thus remained to China.

Who then were 'the Macao people' and 'its inhabitants', so specifically singled out, as described above, as having won this distinction for their city by their long sustained show of loyalty? They were mainly Macanese, who formed the largest part of the Portuguese population of Macao. Many of them were the descendants of a planned — not chance — liaison between Portuguese men and local women. Albuquerque, Portugal's first Governor of its colonies in India, was mainly responsible for this policy of populating Portugal's settlements in the orient. Early in his governorship, it became abundantly evident to him that his country's sparse population could not even continue to supply the men required to man the increasing number and size of her ships, let alone defend her sea routes and at the same time administer, defend and populate her colonies. Nor could Portuguese women be taken out to the colonies in numbers sufficient to make any appreciable difference to the national population requirements there, without at the same time endangering parallel requirements at home. The Albuquerque plan was that the men stationed abroad in the lower ranks of Portugal's services should be encouraged to establish their homes overseas, not by allowing indiscriminate marriages, but by fostering those between couples carefully screened by representatives of both lay and religious bodies. The plan had the full approval of the Roman Catholic Church because it helped to ensure that Portugal's overseas community remained predominantly true to the faith. This Albuquerque policy of controlled intermarriages was one of the main reasons why Portugal's early colonies were so successful, and in Macao it was mainly these local families who, in spite of the social discrimination exercised by some of the European-born Portuguese against them, earned the promotion of Macao's council from *Nobre* to Leal Senado.

Probably the closest modern counterpart of this community honour is the award to Malta of the George Cross for the bravery of her people during the air and sea raids on their island in World War II. Malta was the only British colony to be thus honoured, and Macao was the only one of the four Portuguese Senates overseas to earn the title '*Leal*' from her motherland.

Immediately inside the main door of the *Senado da Câmara* is a large vestibule from which doors and stairways lead to the offices and meeting chambers of the Council. High on the walls of this vestibule are a number of granite commemorative stones and a small one on the south wall closest to the south-west corner is of special interest because it refers to the period of Portugal's submission to Spain.

REINAD EELIPE
4° NOSO. SOR. E
SENDO CAPT.ᴹ DE
STA FORTALEZA
FRCᵒ DE SOUZA
DE CASTRO SE
FES ESTE BEL
VARTE NAER A
D. 1633

DURING THE REIGN OF
PHILIP IV, OUR LORD,
AND BEING CAPTAIN
OF THIS FORTRESS,
FRANCISCO
DE SOUZA DE CASTRO,
THIS BULWARK WAS
MADE IN THE YEAR
AD 1633

Centre: Granite commemorative stone high up on the south inner wall of the vestibule of the Senado da Câmara. On the upper part of the stone is carved the equi-limbed cross used by the Iberian Crusaders and explorers, and below this is carved the inscription in which many abbreviations are used. It has not been possible to approach close enough to the stone to see whether the spelling EELIPE for FELIPE is a painter's or a sculptor's error. **Left:** *The wording of the Portuguese inscription.* **Right:** *An English translation of the wording.*

The year 1633 was the twelfth year of the reign of Philip IV over the dual kingdoms of Spain and Portugal and it was the seventh year before Portugal threw off the Spanish yoke. The inscription, written in Portuguese by a Portuguese fortress commander and referring to the King of Spain as 'Our Lord', can have only one interpretation: that in Macao in 1633 it was recognized that they were under the sovereignty of Spain. Philip IV was reputed to be 'an amiable prince, not interested in politics', and such a tribute as this inscription would have been spontaneous rather than officially prompted, and would indicate that the Spanish yoke lay easily on Portuguese shoulders in Macao and was not one of oppression. Philip's character is indicated by his statement during Portugal's struggle for freedom:

These evil events have been caused by your sins and mine in particular . . . I believe that God our Lord is angry and irate with me and my realms on account of many sins and particularly on account of mine.

It has not been possible to establish the identity of the fortress mentioned in the inscription, but the history of the stone is that it was discarded when the fort was disbanded or when a portion of it was being rebuilt. It subsequently came into the possession of Juan Lecaroz, a Spanish resident in Macao who preserved it in his garden, apparently for the patriotic or sentimental reason that the inscription referred to a Spanish king.

EARLY CHINESE RELATIONS WITH MACAO

THERE CAN BE NO DOUBT that when the Portuguese first established themselves at Ah-ma-kao, they firmly believed that there had been a complete and permanent transfer to them by the Chinese of the land for the settlement and of its surrounding peninsula (and perhaps even of a part of Heung Shan Island also). The local mandarins too seemed for some time to be quite content to let the Portuguese believe this to be so, for they certainly took no obvious steps to indicate the contrary to be the case. It was not until it became apparent that the scourge of piracy had been decisively checked in the waters around Macao that the mandarins gradually began to encroach on what the Portuguese believed had become their sovereign rights and territory. The Chinese were probably encouraged in this policy of encroachment or re-entry by the political weakness of Portugal during her sixty years of Spanish dominance which began

only twenty-three years after Macao was founded — another part of the big price Portugal paid for these six lost decades.

Whatever history may decide are the true circumstances and details of the cession of Macao to Portugal, it is clear that for some time after 1557, it was accepted as a fact by the local officials of both nations concerned. While it is true that neither Lisbon nor Peking took any immediate steps to recognize Macao's new status, that omission may well be due to the feeling that as long as far-distant Macao did not become a political or financial embarrassment to either capital city, they were both content to leave its development to its own devices and resources, and the solution of its international problems to their own provincial representatives on the spot. This being so, it may well be that the cause of the breakdown of these amicable arrangements so soon after cession was initially due to clashes between provincial officials and had nothing to do with centrally controlled national policy; this would automatically become involved later. This explanation certainly fits the picture for in the early stages of the Portuguese occupation of Macao, the local situation was one of true symbiosis, each provincial national group deriving from the mutual association benefits which they could not possibly have enjoyed in their separate existences.

A local example of the way in which the two communities worked together initially was provided by their customs services. Before the coming of the Westerners, South China's overseas trade was mainly with the countries of the present South East Asia, plus the Philippines, the East Indies and other places as far west as India. Canton was the main China terminal of this trade and the anchorage in the Macao Roads off the island of Taipa was one of its subsidiary estuary ports. But since there was no Chinese official resident on the Macao peninsula in those early days, the Chinese customs formalities with the overseas junks had to be discharged by an officer of the staff of the District Magistrate (Heungshan Hien) stationed at Tsin Shan, the chief provincial town in the Heung Shan district, close to where the international border was later established. This officer was known as the Sub-Magistrate (Tsotang) and he used to journey into Macao whenever he had official duties to perform there. On such occasions he was always accorded the honours on arrival due to a foreign official of his rank. In the young settlement of Macao, the Portuguese organized their own customs service to deal with the ships of their overseas trade; these ships used Macao's Outer and Inner Harbours, and were attended to entirely independently of the Chinese customs unless the ship, or part of its cargo, was destined for China. Then the two customs services worked together and the customs dues were collected jointly.

This co-operation between the two national services was found by both to be more valuable than ever when Macao built up her large trade with Japan. This arrangement was especially valuable to the Chinese when Japan closed down all her trade with China. As this prohibition did not apply to the Portuguese, China profited from the fact that Macao was not Chinese for she was able to continue to participate in the Japan trade without having to resort to clandestine methods, and to share with her co-partner not only the duties involved but the duties accruing. But once a convenient procedure such as this is established, it is well-nigh impossible to stop it even when the real need for it no longer exists. This is what happened in 1639 when Japan extended her trade prohibition to the Portuguese

as well. This did away with the need for such a high measure of customs co-operation in Macao, but the Chinese were loath to forgo the footing they had established there. There is, however, this to be said in favour of the continued functioning of a Chinese customs representative in Macao; the loss of Macao's Japanese trade was compensated for by the increase in European trade with Canton, since many of the overseas ships found it convenient to make their first stop on the China mainland at the Macao Roads. They also found it financially worthwhile to conduct, through the Tsotang there, all the preliminary arrangements necessary for entry to the Pearl River, including for example payment of measurement dues, pilot fees and for the Small Chop required for the approach to Bocca Tigris. This ultimately turned out to be to Macao's advantage when the trade of the other European maritime powers increased so much that it overshadowed all other trade in South China. Scores of their ships per season made Macao a routine port of call, and when they established their factories and homes for their families there as well, Macao found herself no longer entirely financially dependent on her own dwindling trade. But even before that, the Portuguese in Macao turned their close association with the Chinese customs staff to their own financial advantage by arranging, through gifts and profit sharing, for permission to visit Canton and trade in materials which the Chinese themselves were prohibited from exporting. This trade of course was done without Peking's knowledge or approval and came to an end in the 1680s, but it must be taken into consideration when assessing the advantages and the disadvantages to the Portuguese of the Tsotang system.

The Macao customs problem ceased to be a provincial one involving only local officials when

Peking, in 1685, decentralized her customs affairs by appointing a member of the Imperial Household Department as Superintendent of Maritime Customs in Kwangtung, with control over the central offices in Canton and over the provincial customs personnel throughout the delta and estuary ports, including Macao. The main duty of this appointee was to ensure that the maximum of the Emperor's share of the customs revenues reached Peking, especially as an increase in foreign trade was envisaged with Canton. This was to be achieved by ceasing to remit the revenue through the Kwangtung provincial government, and sending it direct to the Bureau of Finance (sometimes referred to as the Revenue Board) in Peking. The Bureau was known to foreigners as the Ho-pu or Hu-pu, which may account for this official being referred to in English as the 'Hoppo' and in Portuguese as the 'Opu'.

As can be imagined, this appointment was not popular with the local provincial officials for it deprived them of the lucrative squeeze from merchants and of the not inconsiderable percentage of the taxes passing through their hands which never reached the Governor in Canton. Nevertheless, the local officials did have the advantage over the Hoppo in having personal contact with the smugglers and fishermen who were the only people having an intimate knowledge of the maze of winding waterways that dissected the hundreds of square miles of mangrove swamps into the innumberable delta islands at the mouth of the Canton River. The coming of the Hoppo thus resulted in the establishment of a clandestine liaison between the provincial officials and smugglers against the Emperor's direct representative. This was the liaison which a century or so later, provided the distributing system which helped to keep the opium trade alive against the Emperor's orders. Of all the delta ports, Macao was the furthest from Canton (apart from Whampoa, it was the largest) and since the Chinese customs affairs there were under the Tsin Shan provincial official, the Hoppo needed his own separate representative in Macao. Hence in 1688, he took the step, which Macao was powerless to resist, of erecting a landing pier in the Inner Harbour and a customs house on the shore side of the Praia Grande which was built as late as 1738. These were used by Hoppo officers until 1849 when Governor Amaral demolished them and forced all Chinese officials to leave Macao.

This same was later also used by Chinese officers, for. In 1736 a Sub-Magistrate (referred to by Professor Boxer as the Tso-hang) was posted to Macao from the Tsin Shan office. His duties were to exercise the jurisdiction which was claimed by the officials at Tsin Shan over all the Chinese living in Macao. This mandarin gradually encroached on such civic affairs as land purchase, building construction and repairs, until, even if he did not openly control all of the transactions associated with these, he had a big say behind the scenes in granting the permits for them. As can be imagined, the fees — or squeeze — accruing made him one of the most powerful as well as most wealthy officials in Macao.

This subject of Chinese encroachment was mentioned by Sir George Staunton in his account of Macartney's Embassy to China, published in 1794. His comments prompted by some observations he made on the Senado, read:

> In the senate house, which is built of granite, and two stories high, are several columns of the same material, with Chinese characters cut into them, signifying a solemn cession of the place from the Emperor of China. This solid monument is, however, an insufficient guard against the

encroachments of its Chinese neighbours, who
treat the Portuguese very cavalierly; exact duties
sometimes in the port of Macao; punish
individuals within their walls for crimes
committed against Chinese, particularly murder;
...

That 'this solid monument', though built of stone,
could be an 'insufficient' memorial. It was a
prophecy that became all too true, for this historic
piece of granite evidence of the cession of Macao
has now disappeared. When this former senate
house described by Staunton had outlived its
usefulness, it was demolished to make way for the
present building, and J.P. Braga describes how
during its demolition these valuable pieces of history
were destroyed by the stone-breakers and removed.
Whether this was done partly for political reasons
or solely for financial ones is not known.

No discussion on this subject of the
international status of Macao would be complete
without a reference, even though here it must be
but a passing one, to Anders Ljungstedt, a Swedish
merchant who lived for many years in Canton and
Macao in the early nineteenth century. In his book
published in Boston shortly after his death in 1835,
Ljungstedt expressed his doubts concerning the
validity of the Portuguese claims to Macao, and
since then his views have been the subject of more
references and comments than perhaps they really
merit. Many people have uncritically accepted and
repeated his views and many others have violently
opposed them, more out of religious prejudice than
after an unbiased study of them. Obviously, the
one piece of fundamental evidence that could have
settled the problem would have been a signed copy
of the agreement between Peking and Lisbon, but
alas this has never been forthcoming from either

capital. But decrees issued from time to time during
the latter decades of the eighteenth century indicate
clearly what the official Portuguese understanding
of the legal status of the settlement was. Similarly
du Halde, after having access to official Chinese
correspondence of the period (he was 100 years
closer to the period of the cession than Ljungstedt
was) wrote in 1735:

> The Viceroy [of Kwangsi and Kwangtung]
> reported the victory [of the Portuguese over the
> pirates] to the Emperor who issued an edict
> whereby Macao was awarded to the European
> merchants as a place in which they might settle.

After prolonged study of much of the available
evidence on both sides, Boxer concludes that
'nothing very definite has been established'. He
goes on to say that although Padre Gregorio
Goncalves, a secular priest, writing about 1570,
refers to the first settlers of 1555 as unauthorized
squatters, the priest makes no mention of the
traditional story of their help to the Cantonese in
suppressing pirate bands. Boxer adds that 'it is,
however, quite possible that they had done so, if
mainly for their own benefit'. We are thus still
faced with the unsolved problem of under what
conditions 'the Europeans were allowed to establish
themselves at Macao'. Nor is its solution of merely
academic interest only; its solution is in the interests
of international peace in this part of the world, for
if the occupation of Ah-ma-kao by the Portuguese
was by agreement, the subsequent reactions of the
Chinese towards them must be looked upon as
either deliberate encroachments on Portuguese
sovereign territory, or as a means of gradually
extricating herself from an agreement that was no
longer to her liking or which she never intended to

keep. This would not be the only example in her history of central disapproval of provincial action resulting in a train of purposeful acts planned to lead to the subsequent repudiation of the offending agreement. We shall deal later with China's repudiation of her obligation regarding Canton as a Treaty Port under the Treaty of Nanking in 1843, and how this made the war that followed the *Arrow* incident of 8 October 1856 inevitable. Every country has the right to change its mind, but it has no right to distort historical facts in order to justify the change.

MACAO'S STATUS

FROM THE FOREGOING DISCUSSION of Macao's early days, it is clear that the claim that the Chinese did not release their customs control over the Ah-ma-kao territory when they handed it over to the Portuguese in 1557 is misleading. When the Portuguese settled in Macao, there was no overseas trade to warrant any Chinese customs control there. It was not until the Portuguese brought the trade there that the Chinese customs officials began to take an interest in it, and even then they did not collect revenue in Macao for goods being imported into the settlement itself. They were interested only in such merchandise as was destined for China via Macao, and a special official came into the settlement from Tsin Shan for the purpose, an arrangement which was of mutual advantage to both the local Chinese and to Macao. To the former, it was a means of bringing additional revenue to the Heung Shan district office, and to the latter because much of the increasing foreign trade was attracted to Macao since it proved to be the most convenient of all the estuary ports for the initial

customs formalities for ships bound for Canton. It was not until Macao had become a flourishing and convenient overseas terminus for occidental trade that the Hoppo decided to post a customs officer there and it was this move that heralded the end of the international honeymoon and the beginning of the long period of disharmony between Peking and Lisbon concerning Macao.

Two other historical pointers which are often quoted as indicating the unbroken Chinese ownership of Macao are the official influence continuously exercised by the mandarins over Macao and the payment of 'ground-rent'.

It was during the period of the domination of Spain over Portugal that the payment of 'ground-rent' by Macao to the Chinese was first mentioned. This, however, does not constitute conclusive evidence of uninterrupted Chinese ownership of the territory, for the transaction could just as easily have started as 'gifts' to facilitate dealings with Chinese officials, and later to have come to be looked upon as a right and to have been given the inoffensive name of 'ground-rent'. These points are well illustrated by the minutes of the Macao Senate budget meeting held on 22 January 1691; these referred to:

> . . . the excessive disbursements which continually have to be made to the Chinese for the peace and preservation of this place, and also the payment of the ground-rent which this year has been increased by 100 taels, . . .

The other historical pointer to the unbroken Chinese ownership of Macao mentioned was the continued influence exercised by mandarins over Macao's internal affairs. How soon after the establishment of the Portuguese settlement this interference began is not clear, but in the very early

1600s, the Chinese forced the Portuguese to abandon the building of the Barra Fort on the pretext that it might be used as a defence against them. The next specific case was in 1621 when the Chinese demanded that buildings being erected by the Jesuits on Green Island in the Inner Harbour should be demolished. The Jesuits had previously partially fortified The Monte. Again, the grounds for this encroachment on Macao's sovereign affairs was that the building was intended for military purposes, an accusation that both the Senate and the Rector of the Jesuit College, Padre Gabriel de Mattos, strongly refuted. In the end, the Senate found they had to agree to the Chinese demand which was accompanied by threats to use blockade and force. This decision was not taken until the whole situation, including the question of cession, was debated from every angle. The Chinese case was strongly contested at every point by the Jesuit Rector; he attacked those members of the Senate who favoured compliance with the Chinese demands because they believed that 'this land in which we live is not ours but belongs to the Emperor of China'. Padre Gabriel denied this, claiming that Macao was as much Portuguese as Cochin and other territories in India, and dismissed the argument concerning ground-rent by likening it to the rent paid by Portuguese landowners to a duke. However, his main contention regarding the immediate problem was that the Chinese were bluffing and that a strong line against them would settle the issue. Professor Boxer concludes his comments on the issue thus:

> The senators rejected the bellicose Jesuit's arguments and settled the dispute as they settled all similar difficulties with the Chinese authorities by employing a mixture of simulated obedience, secret compromise, and bribery.

He further adds to these comments, those of António Bocarro, written in 1635:

> The peace that we have with the king of China is as he likes it, for since this place is so far from India, and since he has such vastly greater numbers of men than the most that the Portuguese could possibly assemble there, never did we think of breaking with him whatever serious grievances we may have had because the Chinese have only to stop our food-supplies to ruin our city, since there is no other place nor means of obtaining any.

The authorities in Goa and Lisbon were just as critical of the Senate for their policy of appeasement as the Rector was, but in fairness to the Senators, it must be remembered that it was the people on the spot who would have to suffer the consequences of any strong action they took. Such consequences would be certain to include an embargo on all food supplies from China to the community, and this could only be successfully resisted by the colony if it had the backing of force which Portugal, for many reasons, was not able to supply. It was not until 1849 that Macao found a patriot strong, capable and courageous enough to resist the increasing demands of the Chinese; but in the meantime, the Chinese encroachments increased in frequency, intensity and scope.

STRUGGLE FOR COLONY STATUS

THE FOURTH AND FIFTH DECADES of the nineteenth century witnessed big changes in international relations and in foreign trade in Macao and Canton.

Firstly, in the early 1830s, there was the emergence of the English free merchants and the passing of the East India Company, followed in the latter part of that decade by the stepping up of the troubles between the foreigners and Chinese, highlighted by the opium climax and the outbreak of the first Sino-British War. The next decade saw the coming of peace and the spate of foreign treaties with China, one of which — the Sino-American Treaty — was closely associated with Macao. It was negotiated and signed there in the Kun Yum Tong (觀音堂), the Buddhist temple of the Goddess of Mercy.

Unlike that of Ah-Ma, this temple lies outside the old city limits and is now surrounded by what may well be described as the garden suburb of Mong Há, which has replaced the earlier Mong Há village. The original village was the first habitation known to exist on the peninsula, and is said to have been built by early migrants from Fukien; but unlike the Fukien boat-people who came later and founded the fishing village of Ah-ma-kao, the Mong Há people were tillers of the soil and chose for the site of their cultivations the rich valley nestling between Guia Hill and The Monte to the south, and the low-lying hills of Montanha Russa and Meersburg to the north. For centuries, Mong Há village remained but an unpretentious collection of peasant houses around and alongside the rude altar built by their founders and dedicated to their Goddess of Mercy, while Ah-ma-kao, on the other hand, developed into a flourishing city. However in the late 1620s, well after the coming of the Portuguese, Mong Há took on a new lease of life and developed into a prosperous village whose people acknowledged their gratitude to their gods by erecting temple buildings around the site of the original altar. Though founded therefore, long before the Temple of Ah-Ma, the buildings of the Temple of Kun Yum date from a much later period

and are good examples of Ming temple architecture. How the architecture and the surroundings of the temple impressed a Cantonese refugee from Nam Hoi (南海) in 1943 during the Second World War is recorded in the inscription on a tablet now in one of the courtyards of the temple. This tablet commemorated the signing in the temple of the above-mentioned Sino-American Treaty, the first to be negotiated between these two countries. It is from this event, rather than from the temple's architecture or its religious associations that it owes its historic interest. In this courtyard near the memorial tablet is a round, stone table said to have been the one at which Viceroy Yi and Caleb Cushing signed the treaty on 3 July 1844. The table is small (4′ in diameter) but substantial, and the surrounding

A view of one of the eastern courtyards in the Temple of Kun Yum, showing in the foreground, the round stone table at which the Sino-American Treaty of 1844 was signed; in the background, a tablet carrying a Chinese inscription carved in 1943, ninety-nine years after the event it commemorates.

stone benches are extremely uncomfortable, but the seated signatories could not have been half as uncomfortable as their Portuguese hosts must have been when they stood on their own territory and watched their American guests receive from the Chinese 'most favoured nation' privileges, while they themselves had not yet been able to extract from them an official recognition of even their own existing rights and status, let alone additional favours.

For the next decade or two after the signing of the treaty, Macao's position *vis-a-vis* China remained as unsatisfactory as ever; in fact it was not until 1862 that Portugal was able to persuade China to meet her at the conference table in order to regularize in writing Macao's status which China had refused to recognize ever since 1557. But even then China evaded the ratification of this agreement and it was 1887 before she could again be brought to the conference table to draw up the agreement which was finally ratified by both countries in December of the Rat Year, and on which Portugal's present claim to Macao rests. In the meantime, Macao continued the uphill struggle towards her goal, and two statues, one of a naval officer born in Portugal and the other of a gunner officer born in Macao, commemorate the deeds of the two men mainly responsible for bringing Macao safely through one of the most critical periods of its history. This was in 1849 and between the city's foundation in 1586 and that date, Macao's position had been far from satisfactory; it was also far from static and in the opinion of many Portuguese, it had been steadily deteriorating throughout. Nor were the Chinese alone in the continual acts of ignoring Macao's claim to independent status. The trading companies of the European maritime powers (and from the days of their independence onwards,

the Americans too) all seemed to take it for granted that the trading and other facilities of Macao were theirs for the using, often even without the asking. At times their actions and their reasoning even indicated that they regarded Macao itself as theirs for the taking, if and when it suited them. Macao resisted the threats of the Dutch with force, and those of the British with diplomacy and firmness; the French threat she avoided. Alone of all the major powers the Americans used no threats, but they made such use of their opportunities that their annual shipping tonnage in Macao rapidly became second in size only to the British.

Macao's trouble was a dual one: her weakness in the east and her lack of support from the west. The forces she could bring to bear on pirate bands in the 1550s were useless against peaceful penetration or armed invasion by the great powers of the late 1700s and early 1800s. Ever since the Dutch, French and English had disrupted her trade routes, Portugal was unable to provide anything but the most meagre help to its distant settlements like Macao. It was not that the authorities in Lisbon were disinterested in Macao's welfare; far from it, from time to time they urged Macao to take stronger action locally against China's encroachment on her sovereignty, and where and when possible they did give material help.

The first step taken by Portugal to strengthen Macao's international position was to abolish the intermediate administrative control exercised over her by the Viceroy of Goa, and for Lisbon itself to assume the direct responsibility for the Colony's affairs. This gave Macao's problems a much better chance of consideration at the national level than could ever have been achieved through the Viceroy, distant from Macao's affairs as he was at Goa. The first fruits of this administrative change were hastened by the signing of the Treaty of Nanking after the first Sino-British War. The terms which the Chinese were then forced to give Britain were in such marked contrast to the treatment they were accustomed to mete out to Macao, that the latter was made to appear before the outside world as nothing more than a Chinese vassal state. Portugal was affronted and Macao aggrieved, and with no small amount of justification either, especially when the other European nations demanded the same treatment as Britain was awarded. America, as we have just seen, even carried out her negotiations with the Chinese for this favoured treatment in Macao itself.

JOÃO MARIA FERREIRA DO AMARAL (1805–1849)

WITH THE TERMINATION of the first Sino-British War, Portugal decided it was time for her to re-establish her national position in the Orient as she believed it was intended to be in 1557; her major decisions were to expel all Chinese officials from Macao, to cease paying the annual 'ground-rent' and, in order to combat their loss of trade due to the establishment of the newly opened free port of Hong Kong, it was further decided that Macao should also become a free port. This latter step was taken by royal decree in Lisbon on 20 November 1845 and the task of re-establishing Macao's *de facto* independence from China was given to a new governor, Captain João Maria Ferreira do Amaral.

Amaral was born in 1805 and when but a midshipman in 1823, he first came into prominence as one of Portugal's heroes by his display of outstanding courage and leadership while in command of a storming party near Bahia, Brazil.

During the charge, he lost his right arm, but this misfortune he is reported to have turned to advantage by rallying his men with the exhortation 'Forward, my brave comrades! I have another arm left me still.' It was not until years later, in Macao, that this misfortune was to take its full toll — his life.

Amaral arrived in Macao on 21 April 1846 and assumed a governorship which soon gave evidence that it demanded of him administrative fortitude every bit as great as the bravery he had shown on the battlefield 23 years earlier. On every side he encountered opposition from the Chinese because his instructions from Lisbon included the re-establishment of Macao's recognition as a colony, and from his own Senators and merchants, because they believed that Lisbon's free port decision spelled disaster for Macao; nor did he receive the support he needed and rightly expected from Portugal. He was given no extra funds to pay for the new measures he was to introduce, or to meet the cost of the emergencies they might occasion. One of the emergencies that did arise was the near mutiny of the reinforcements to the garrison who, he found on his arrival, had received no pay for months, nor had any financial provision been made for their payment in the future. Finance was thus Amaral's major problem, but his plans to raise revenue through land and income taxation resulted in only adding to his difficulties for they incensed the Senators who retaliated by sending secret dispatches to Lisbon, adversely criticizing his plans and his actions. On discovering their underhand activities, Amaral acted swiftly and strongly by dissolving the Senate, thus depriving them of their status and power.

His next decision was to abolish the control exercised in Macao by the resident mandarin at the

Chinese custom houses on the Inner and Outer Harbours (Praia Pequena and Praia Grande). Amaral claimed that since Macao was now a free port, this office, originally set up merely on the grounds of convenience, was now redundant. When the Chinese officials refused to close their office, Amaral abolished the post by proclamation on 5 March 1849. On 13 March, when his orders were still disregarded, he expelled the staff and notified the mandarins at Heung Shan that if they ever had occasion in the future to visit Macao, they would be accorded the full honours due to *foreign* officials of their rank and status. They left without creating any further trouble. When however, the Legations to China of France, Spain and the United States chose to make Macao their headquarters rather than Hong Kong while they waited — in vain — for admission to China, the Portuguese reasonably interpreted this as the *de facto* recognition by these countries of her status. All these factors led to a deterioration in the relations between China and Macao, and in Canton public feeling regarding the Portuguese was inflamed, a reward being offered for Amaral's head.

Since Amaral's arrival in Macao he had made a habit of taking an evening ride on horseback to the barrier and back accompanied by his *aide-de-camp*, Lieutenant Leite; this he did in spite of more than one warning from friends that this was unwise and dangerous. On his way back from the barrier on the evening of 22 August 1849, when but a few hundred yards inside the gate a Chinese coolie frightened the Governor's horse with a bamboo pole and then, while the one-armed Amaral was preoccupied in trying to regain control of his horse with the stave, signalled to others waiting hidden nearby. Transferring the bridle reins to his teeth to free his only hand, Amaral tried to draw his pistol but before he could do so, he was set upon by seven more Chinese who, armed with swords, dragged both the Portuguese from their mounts. While Leite (though also armed) made a rather ignominious escape, Amaral, in keeping with his character, put up a courageous resistance and the examination of the marks subsequently found on the site bore eloquent testimony to the ferocity of the attack, and the valour with which Amaral made his last stand.

The memorial which depicts Amaral's fight, the result of which had been so cruelly predestined in the action at Bahia a quarter of a century before, stood on the Outer Harbour reclamation, and is Macao's most eloquent statue.

Amaral's assassins made good their escape, the blood trail of his mutilated head and hand indicating the route they took; it led through the Barrier Gate. From here they sped to Canton to collect the reward offered for Amaral's assassination taking with them the gruesome evidence which was to substantiate their claim. Their presence in Canton together with their exhibits was to prove to be an embarrassment to the Chinese officials later because, when the Portuguese protest was made, and especially when it was strongly supported by the British Plenipotentiary and the American, French and Spanish Ministers then in South China, the Chinese first defence was official ignorance of the whole affair.

In the meantime in Macao, as was only to be expected, with its Senate dissolved and its autocratic Governor dead, affairs were thrown into confusion. Responsibility for the administration of public affairs was assumed by a small group of senior officials who appealed to foreign representatives for

The memorial to Governor Amaral which stood on the southern corner of the reclamation overlooking the Outer Harbour, at the elbow bend of Avenida do Amizade. The monument was approximately 50 feet high and consisted of an equestrian status 15 feet high, resting on a thick quadrangular table which in turn was supported at its four corners by substantial cylindrical columns. Affixed to the bases of these columns were two shields carved with royal arms in bas-relief, and two marble tablets carrying Portuguese inscriptions. The monument was designed and the statue sculptured by Maximileão Alves. It was originally placed in the Praia Grande and was transferred after the reclamation was formed.

The statue was removed and shipped to Portugal in 1993. The reasons for this have been variously given as an improvement to the feng shui *of the nearby Hotel Lisboa, and as a response to a request for the removal of this symbol of colonialism by the Chinese government, in light of the impending transfer of administration in 1999.*

help should the Chinese attack their defenceless colony. In response to this appeal, two American naval vessels, the *Plymouth* and the *Dolphin*, took up positions to guard Macao's sea approaches, and HMS's *Amazon* and *Medea* landed marines to protect Portuguese civilians and property, as well as their own nationals.

On investigation of the course of events at the Barrier Gate, it was found that most of the guards who had let the assassins through unhindered had fled their post leaving only a corporal and two privates in charge; these three the Portuguese took into custody and used as hostages in the ensuing negotiations. When the Portuguese demanded the return of Amaral's head and hand, the Chinese first denied any knowledge of them and counter-demanded the release of their three soldiers; but when the Portuguese made it quite clear that the return of the Amaral remains was an essential preliminary to any negotiations, the Chinese claimed that they had executed the murderer but had failed to ascertain first where he had buried the remains. Eventually, they were returned on 16 January 1850, but only after the Chinese had raised many side issues and had failed to keep earlier promises for their return. They were finally brought to the Praia Grande by two Chinese in a hired junk and there, in the complete absence of any ceremony, they were handed over in an open bucket. They had, however, been previously well preserved, and there was certainly no evidence of their having been earlier buried by the assassin as the Chinese originally claimed. Amaral's head and hand were laid alongside his body then reposing in the Government House Chapel, and were later encoffined together and removed to the Church of St. Francis, where the last funeral rites were performed, and then later taken to Lisbon where they were finally laid to rest in the *Cemitério dos Prazeres*.

Amaral's political ideals and methods may have laid him open to the accusation of being inexperienced in the field of Asian politics, but in appraising this, we should need to know his briefing and how far he was led to believe he could rely on help from Goa or Portugal. In any case, no one can gainsay his bravery, not only in the face of his country's enemies, but in the face of his political enemies amongst his own people. Nor can his steadfastness of purpose or his loyalty to his cause be denied. For these he paid the price and it was probably better that way, for he may well have had to face a political death at the hands of his opponents had he continued with his reforms in Macao as he had begun. As it was he died as a national martyr and not as a political sacrifice, and he died early enough in his career for a contemporary Hong Kong newspaper to write this of him, which even if it goes further than our present-day knowledge of him would permit us to do, it does indicate the type of man he must have been:

> . . . a nobler spirit than his never animated its tenement of clay, and he wanted nothing but opportunity and a wider sphere to have achieved a name equal to any in the annals of the age.

One thing we can say with certainty however, is that neither his life nor his death was in vain for many of the reforms he introduced into the governing of Macao were retained permanently, and the example he set in fighting his enemies was followed by yet another Macao hero, and with what results we shall discuss in the next section. In the meantime, we must listen to the voice of yet one more Macao stone which speaks of Amaral.

This is a natural granite boulder whose ovoid outcrop is about 4 feet high, 6 feet wide and 10 feet long, its greater axis lying east and west. It is to be found in a small neglected grass plot in the Estrada do Arco, not a very great distance from the place where the outnumbered and outmanoeuvred Amaral made his last bid for life. This probably accounts for the traditional story that the carving on it is to commemorate this last stand. This belief is given all the more credence by a statement which has been widely repeated that the boulder has the date of Amaral's assassination '22.8.1849' carved upon it.

The stone shows clearly that the date on the stone does not refer to the year of Amaral's death (1849), nor is there any reference made to either a day or a month in the carving. Another reason therefore must be found for this stone being associated in the minds of Macao's people with Amaral. It will be found in the history of the Macao events of 1848 — the date carved on the stone — or of the period just prior to it, certainly not after it; it therefore can have no association with Amaral's death in 1849.

In 1848, the economic measures introduced by Amaral began to bear fruit, and the financial crisis showed signs of abating as more and more of the economic and administrative threads woven around Macao by China were severed. The most significant

A general view of the 'Amaral' stone, showing the Portuguese coat of arms carved on its western side.

of the measures taken in 1848 was that of cleaning up a morass which existed in an area between the city walls near the Campo and the Portas do Cerco at the boundary. A part of this area was an insanitary mixture of Chinese shacks and refuse dumps, of paddy fields and piggeries, while on the islands of higher ground were ill-kept burial sites where packs of pariah dogs and pigs roved in search of food however unsavoury.

These Chinese squatters resented Amaral's 'interference' and in this resentment they were actively supported by the Chinese mandarins at Heung Shan, who at a quite recent 'convention', of 1749 had forced the Macao Senate to agree that the area between the city hall and the existing boundary really belonged to China, and had subsequently called upon the Chinese living there to pay their land taxes to them and not to the Portuguese. The mandarins had erected a tablet on the Macao side of the border setting out the articles of this 'convention' of 1749 and reminding the Chinese of their obligations. Amaral refused to recognize the validity

of these articles, or of their applicability to the situation, and as far as the Portuguese were concerned, he saw in the articles only another act of perfidy by the Senate, and he regarded the erection of the tablet as an affront to the national dignity of Portugal. He therefore removed the tablet and at the same time reasserted Portuguese authority and active control over the whole area.

The Heung Shan mandarin retaliated by publishing a notice on 20 April to the effect that all Chinese residents of Macao must pay land taxes to the government of China and not to the Macao authorities, and in default, threatened capital punishment and confiscation of half their property. On 5 May, Amaral countered this move with a proclamation to the effect that the territory under discussion was Portuguese and that rents of all land within the border must be paid to the Portuguese authorities in Macao and not to the Chinese officials at Heung Shan. Amaral's removal of the Chinese tablet demonstrated how easily an artificial monument could be destroyed and this must have made him decide that the situation called for the erection of a more permanent monument that would proclaim to all observers that the entire territory within Macao's borders was Portuguese, and what could be more permanent than a large, natural rock, its base buried firmly and deep in the soil of Macao, and what could be more explicitly vocal and to the point than the Portuguese coat of arms and the date — 1848?

VICENTE NICOLAU DE MESQUITA (1818–1880)

FOR THE FIRST TWO days after Amaral's death, fear reigned among the population of Macao in spite of the protection provided by the British and American naval craft. But these craft were not there to defend the border and so when, on 25 August, Chinese troops massed in their fort at Passaleão, known also as Pak Lan Shan, and opened fire on the barrier, it looked as though Macao, with its grossly inadequate defence forces, might well suffer the same fate which some of the earlier Portuguese enclaves in China did.

When the position, as viewed by the elders of the disorganized community, appeared to grow more and more hopeless, a young Macao-born gunner subaltern, Vicente Nicolau de Mesquita, courageously — and foolheartedly, as most people at the time thought — volunteered to deal with the threat to their families and their homes by dislodging the Chinese from the fort, on condition that he be allowed to choose his own party of men. Without any faith in this wild scheme, the Portuguese leaders, probably because they had no plans of their own, ultimately gave it their blessing, and while some citizens from neighbouring high ground watched Mesquita and his men sally forth

on their mission, most of their compatriots waited in the city in fear and suspense.

The Chinese fire from the fort was wild and Mesquita's party was able to get within howitzer range without sustaining any casualties; his first shot (and last too, because the recoil broke one of the gun wheels) fell in the fort where the defenders were massed thickest, and caused such carnage that the Chinese fled in panic, taking as many of their dead and wounded with them as they could. Mesquita of course was ignorant of the effect of this shot, so with his gun out of action he was faced with the choice of either charging the fort or retreating. He chose the former, and even when his men subsequently blew the magazine in the fort, their friends in Macao were still uncertain as to their fate until they saw a Portuguese flag flutter from the ramparts. But this relief was only momentary, for on closer observation it was noticed that the national flag had been hoisted upside down and this distress signal threw the city into further consternation. Help was requested from the British naval ships in the harbour and more marines were landed in case the invader gained entrance to the city, for the handful of Portuguese troops at the barrier could not possibly hold up such a large Chinese force if they launched a determined attack. It was some time before the dramatic tension was relieved by a messenger sent by Mesquita with the welcome news of victory, and when eventually he and his men had completed their military mission to their own satisfaction, it was an hilariously happy and relieved city that welcomed back the gallant head who had saved them from almost certain destruction. Their leader, the impetuous and inexperienced youth, unknown a few hours before, had now become a national hero to be remembered for all time.

The British marines remained ashore until the next day, but after visiting the ruins of the Chinese fort, and assuring themselves and the people of Macao that the threat to the city no longer existed, they were withdrawn aboard their ships. Meanwhile the citizens of Macao, having at last thrown off the yoke of mandarindom, now openly assumed before China and the world the status of a colony, the status to which the Portuguese maintained they had been entitled, but had been steadily losing, over the past two centuries. Under the leadership of Bishop Mata, they set about the formidable task of rehabilitation. It is understandable that one of their first projects was to demolish the Chinese barrier gate with its offending admonition: 'Dread our greatness, and respect our virtue', and replace it on the Portuguese side by a triumphal arch, the *Portas do Cerco,* on which is inscribed the less bombastic exhortation in Portuguese: 'Honour thy country, for thy country regards thee'.

But what of their hero to whom they owed their continued existence and freedom? Apart from the immediate expressions of gratitude and the presentation of a sword of honour made by a grateful community to Mesquita, his bravery never received the official recognition it was generally considered to deserve. Because he was locally born, he found his slow and inadequate promotion so much more pointed and more difficult to bear, with the result that he suffered a severe nervous breakdown. Following his recovery, he was given command of a fort on Taipa Island but it was not until after some years in this backwater that he was promoted to the rank of Colonel. However, a further mental relapse ultimately forced his permanent retirement. Family difficulties then ensured which only aggravated the situation, and when appeals to the Bishop and Governor for help were fruitless, in a fit of madness

he slew his wife and daughter and then committed suicide. In these circumstances, the Governor refused to accord him the honour of a military funeral, nor would the Bishop allow him to be buried in consecrated ground. This persecution of the dead hero was even extended to his friends, and, as an example of the extent to which the Portuguese officials of church and state carried their persecution, it is recorded that the Commandant of the Police was removed from his command for being amongst the hundreds of citizens who accompanied the remains of Mesquita to his ignominious grave.

It was many years before these injustices to this brave man were removed. The first step towards his ultimate reinstatement was taken by the Portuguese Consul in Hong Kong in 1884 when he proposed that funds be collected to enable a suitable memorial to be raised to Mesquita. In May 1898, a commission recommended that the 400th anniversary of the first Portuguese contact by sea with India should be commemorated by erecting monuments to both Amaral and Mesquita. This proposal naturally involved the church and it took another twelve years of negotiations before it was possible to take the memorial project any further. But at long last, the same view prevailed that whatever might be the legal or religious opinion concerning Mesquita's final acts, the fact remains that his exploits in 1849 were decisive in the preservation of the community and deserve public commemoration. So, in conformity with popular opinion, Mesquita was reinstated by both civil and church authorities and on 28 August 1910, his remains were reinterred in the *Cemitério de S. Miguel,* and a white marble memorial now marks his last resting place in the first row immediately on the left of the entrance to the cemetery from *Estrada do Cemitério.*

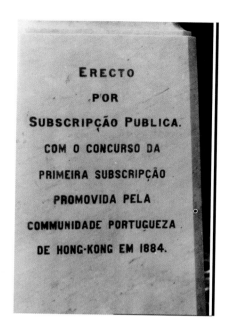

The memorial to Colonel Mesquita over his grave in the public cemetery of St. Michael.

The English translations of the Portuguese inscription read as follows:

Front
In memory of Vicente Nicolau de Mesquita, heroic defender of Macao on 25 August 1849.

West side
Erected by subscriptions to a public fund originated by the Portuguese community of Hong Kong in 1884.

East side
Born on 9 July 1818. Captured Passaleão on 25 August 1849. Died on 20 March 1880. Reinterred 28 August 1910, with full honours, military and ecclesiastical.

Front
A 'MEMORIA
DE
VICENTE NICOLAU
DE MESQUITA
HEROICO DEFENSOR
DE MACAU EM
25 DE AGOSTO DE 1849

West side
ERECTO
POR SUBSCRIPÇÃO PUBLICA
COM O CONCURSO DA
PRIMEIRA SUBSCRIPÇÃO
PROMOVIDA PELA
COMMUNIDADE
PORTUGUEZA
DE HONG-KONG EM 1884

East side
NASCEU EM 9–7–1818
TOMOU PASSALEÃO EM
25–8–1849
FALLECEU EM 20–3–1880
FOI TRANSLADADO EM
28–8–1910
TEVE N'ESSE DIA AS
HONRAS
MILITARES
E
ECCLESIASTICAS

The inscriptions and their English translations read as follows:

(Upper)

Homenagem da Colonia ao Heroico Macanese Coronel Vicente Nicolau de Mesquita 25 de Agosto de 1849

A tribute from the Colony to a Macanese Hero Colonel Vicente Nicolau de Mesquita 25 August 1849

(Lower)

Este monumento, erigido per subscrição publica e auxilio do Governo da Colonia, foi inaugurado por ocasião das festas comemorativas do Duplo Centenário da Fundação e Restauração de Portugal.
24 de Junho de 1940.
Oferta do Leal Senado.

This monument, erected by public subscription and with the help of the Governor of the Colony, was unveiled on the occasion of the celebrations of two centennial anniversaries of the restoration of freedom to Portugal.
24 June 1940
The gift of the Leal Senado.

Alongside this memorial lie the mortal remains of three of his sisters, Balbina (1817–1868), Rosaline (1839–1859) and Leopoldina Rosa (1842–1937). They lie in a tomb which as recently as 1947 was rebuilt by the Leal Senado in homage to the memory of the hero of Passeleão. A marble tablet attached to the top of the tomb gives the names of the three 'beloved ones' and another on the end gives the history of the tomb's reconstruction.

The final steps in Mesquita's public reinstatement were taken in Macao, when, as part of the celebrations connected with the 300th anniversary of Portugal's liberation from the Spanish yoke (1580–1640), a statue of Macao's hero was set up in the centre of the city he bravely saved in 1849. Standing about 22 feet high overall, the memorial, the work of a Portuguese sculptor, Maximileão Alves, was erected in the Largo do Senado directly opposite and facing the Leal Senado. It depicted Mesquita in the act of drawing his sword to lead a charge such as he might well have done at Passaleão.

The Mesquita memorial in the Largo do Senado consisted of a substantial fluted column roughly rectangular in section and 12 feet in height, standing on a granite stepped podium and surmounted by a 10 feet high bronze statue of the hero. The column carried two inscriptions, one engraved on a marble shield attached to the front of the column above a segment of a carved wreath, and the other carved on the granite podium, also on the front facing the Leal Senado. It was destroyed after the events of 1–2–3 December 1966, but still proclaiming its message through its inscriptions. Note the broken windows in the Leal Senado behind the plinth, which was ransacked by rioters at the same time as the statue was removed.

During the '1–2–3' disturbances in December 1966 which caused great and long-lasting harm to Macao, the statue met an ignominious end. Youthful rioters, unable to recognize and reverence bravery unless it be exhibited in a cause of which they approve, tore the Mesquita monument from its pedestal, in addition to sacking the Leal Senado. It was then deposited near the public lavatories on Avenida de Almeida Ribeiro, and daubed with the Chinese legend reading 'This is where you belong'. Unadorned by its statue however, the pedestal probably speaks more eloquently and excites more attention to its inscriptions than when it carried its rather inelegant personification of Mesquita preparing for action against the fort at Passeleão.

In February 1967, probably because the inscription was too frank a reminder of the glories of the colonial past, the pedestal of the memorial was removed as well, and it was decided to replace it by a fountain surrounded by lawns and flowering shrubs. The latter have already been installed but far from removing Mesquita's name from the memories of all loyal Portuguese, the shrubs and lawns will keep his name in their minds, forever fresh and forever green. The fountain has since been replaced as well, and the entire Largo do Senado has been tiled and pedestrianized. Mesquita's only other memorial is in the broad avenue named after him in the north of the city, Avenida de Coronel Mesquita.

FROM COLONY TO PROVINCE

DESPITE THE SACRIFICE of Amaral and the heroism of Mesquita, Macao had to endure the non-recognition of her colony status by the Chinese for another three or four decades. Portugal, however, made a definite step towards this goal in 1862 when she achieved her ambition to sit at the negotiation table with China. Ever since the Sino-British Treaty of Nanking of 1843, she had watched with covetous eyes other Western countries, one after another, succeed in reaching a trade agreement with China. Now, thanks greatly to the strong support of France, it was her turn.

On 13 August 1862, a treaty between China and Portugal was signed in Tientsin. This was basically a trade agreement, but it contained two important clauses as far as Macao's status was concerned. Article II is the usual clause of annullment of earlier agreements, and it refers to Macao as 'formerly in the Province of Canton',

while Article III implies definite recognition of the status of the 'Governor-General of Macao' and therefore of Macao itself. It reads:

> The Governor General of Macao, in his capacity of Plenipotentiary of His Most Faithful Majesty in China, may visit the Court of Peking every year should important affairs render it necessary. If in the future the Government of His Majesty the Emperor of China shall allow the Plenipotentiary of any other Foreign nation to reside permanently at Peking, besides those who have already their Representatives there, the Envoy of His Most Faithful Majesty may consider such permission as extending to himself, and avail of it should he deem convenient.

The Treaty (Article LIV) also laid down that the ratifications were to be exchanged at Tientsin within two years from the date of signature. This was never done and it looks as though the Chinese never intended that it should be done, for the officials throughout the country as well as all the Chinese who had anything to do with foreign trade in South China, were unanimously against Portugal's claim to sovereignty over Macao and its waters. The Chinese therefore quietly opposed the ratification of the treaty of 1862, and the time clause (Article LIV) provided them with a convenient way out. They had only to find excuses for postponing the exchange of copies of the ratified treaty at Tientsin for longer than two years and the whole treaty automatically became null and void and if still wanted after that date, it would have to be negotiated again in its entirety.

This is exactly what happened. China found excuse after excuse for not being able to ratify the 1862 treaty, and Portugal had to wait for almost another quarter of a century after 1864 before a further opportunity of reviving the matter presented itself. Interestingly enough the further opportunity arose out of the opium problem, not out of attempts to abolish the traffic but to tighten its control so that, as far as China was concerned, she could get her fair share of the opium revenue, much of which was then going to corrupt officials in the Hoppo's department and to smugglers.

In June 1886, a joint Sino-British commission was appointed which ultimately advised that the responsibility for the administration of the import of opium into China be transferred from the Hoppoate to the Chinese Maritime Customs. This was agreed by the two nations concerned but it was obvious that the new procedure could not be completely successful unless Portugal was included in the agreement.

Here was Portugal's opportunity and it was China who took the initiative in negotiating for her co-operation. In 1887, China sent a diplomatic mission to Lisbon, and in it the Superintendent of the Chinese Maritime Customs — Sir Robert Hart — was represented by J.D. Campbell, a senior British member of the Customs Service. As a result, representatives of His Most Faithful Majesty, the King of Portugal, and of His Imperial Majesty the Emperor of China, agreed on the following four points:

- a treaty 'with most favoured nation clause' was to be concluded;
- Macao with its dependencies was to be ceded to Portugal; but
- Macao was not to be alienated by Portugal without agreement with China;
- and Macao was to co-operate in opium work in the same way as at Hong Kong.

A Protocol embodying these four points was drawn up and was signed by the representatives in Lisbon on 26 March 1887; the second Article of this Protocol categorically stated:

> China confirms perpetual occupation and government of Macao and its dependencies by Portugal, as any other Portuguese possession.

Portugal quickly followed up this achievement by sending a special envoy to Peking where a treaty of amity and commerce was drawn up along the lines of the Protocol. There, on 1 December 1887, it was signed by representatives of both countries and became known as the Treaty of Peking, 1887. Portugal's special envoy who signed on her behalf was Macao's former Governor, Thomaz de Souza Roza and it was a happy homecoming both for Macao and himself when he returned with the ratified treaty, whose Article II and III declared:

ii. China confirms, in its entirety, the second Article of the Protocol of Lisbon, relating to the perpetual occupation and government of Macao by Portugal.

iii. Portugal confirms, in its entirety, the third Article of the Protocol of Lisbon, relating to the engagement never to alienate Macao [the Protocol here adds 'and its dependencies'] without previous agreement with China.

It is outside the scope of this work to discuss the ultimate nature of Portugal's sovereignty over Macao, but it is relevant to consider these treaty clauses in relation to Macao's claim to colony status. From the Articles quoted above, it is apparent that Portugal had established the right to govern Macao as her possession, and China had disclaimed any right to a say in such affairs unless they involved an alienation of any part of the Macao territory. After December 1887 therefore, such evidence as ground-rent, the presence of a Chinese custom house or a resident Mandarin in Macao, became irrelevant and of academic interest only. Similarly, however justified China's political activities inside Macao were before that date, after the treaty such activities were regarded as encroachments on Macao's sovereignty. The Treaty of Peking was the culmination of Portugal's long endeavour to establish Macao in the eyes of the world in the status it felt had been agreed upon *de facto* three centuries previously. The lesson this long struggle teaches is that it is only by the exercise of goodwill, and by the presence of integrity and trustworthiness in the approach of **both** parties to a *de jure* agreement, that it can ever become an agreement *de facto*.

This status Macao retained until 15 June 1951 when, by an internal readjustment of her constitution and of her administrative system, she became an Overseas Province, integrated with the State of Portugal. Her affairs are correlated with national policy through the National Assembly in Lisbon in which she is represented by a Macao-elected Deputy, and through the Central Government by its Ministry of Overseas Provinces. The head of the provincial administration is the Governor appointed from Lisbon, and he is assisted by a Government Council and an Executive Council who have complete autonomy as far as the finances of the Province are concerned.

The purely municipal affairs such as police, fire services, public transport and utilities, public markets, etc., are the responsibility of the Senate, now a body with powers greatly curtailed in comparison with those it possessed before Amaral's governorship. The islands of Taipa and Coloane, have a separate municipal administration known as the Municipal Commission of the Insular Dependencies, the members of which are nominated by the Macao Government. It was these islands that the negotiators of the 1887 Protocol had in mind when they referred in Article II to 'Macao and *its dependencies*'. Montalto de Jesus adds to these two more islands, São João and Montanha, stating that on none of these four were Chinese troops allowed to land, although Taipa and Coloane were the only two on which the Portuguese stationed detachments of troops or police guards. This historian further states that in 1890 the officials in Canton provisionally agreed on the water boundaries between Macao and China, a line midway between Green Island and the Lappa coast line in the north of the Inner Harbour, and a line from the east end of the Macao land boundary to the Kao Chow or Nine Islands in the east.

DEPENDENCIES OF TAIPA AND COLOANE ISLANDS

THIS PRESENT-DAY Province of Portugal in the Far East (**Map 1**) therefore consists of the Macao peninsula on which the city itself stands, and its two island dependencies lying a few miles to the south. A third island, Green Island at the northern end of the Inner Harbour, is now no longer an island. It has been joined to the isthmus of the peninsula by a causeway and a reclamation. The peninsula itself is about three miles long with an average breadth of one mile, and it makes a contribution of 2.1 square miles to the Province's total area of six square miles, Taipa being 1.4 and Coloane 2.5 square miles in area. The peninsular is attached by a short and very narrow isthmus, to the large delta island formerly known as Heung Shan (香山). Its main claim to fame is that in one of its villages — Tsuiheng (翠亨) — Sun Yat Sen

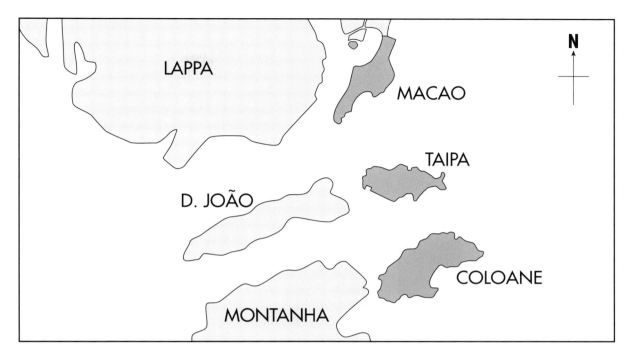

Map 1 Macao, Taipa and Coloane

was born on 12 November 1866; after he became the father and first President of the new Republic of China, the name of this island was changed to Chung Shan (中山), this being one of his adopted names.

Chung Shan was associated with the early settlement of Macao, some writers believing that the whole island was captured by the Portuguese in order to eradicate completely the control of the pirate chief, Chang Si Lao, over the island. It is doubtful whether the Portuguese had sufficient men to accomplish this, but they did bring order and serenity to the whole area and did occupy the

shores *(ribeiras)* of the islands of Chung Shan and Lappa on the western side of the Inner Harbour. The Chinese eventually forced the Portuguese to give these settlements up, but they were not successful in applying the same policy to the use of Taipa and Coloane. In fact, in 1719 it suited China to urge the Portuguese to allow them to build a fort on Taipa to discourage the coming of more European traders, especially the British, and their use of the anchorage there. Macao, fearing it might become another 'Trojan horse', refused the offer. Ljungstedt's account of the occupation of Taipa is that it arose out of the Chinese demand that the Portuguese should 'not suffer foreign ships to lurk among the islands'. In 1732, the Chinese Viceroy of the Two Kwangs made the specific request that he should be kept advised of the details of the ships using the Taipa anchorage — their nationality, their size, their cargo and the object of their voyage. This necessitated permanent and continuous observation and residence on the islands by the Portuguese, and led to the permanent occupation of the islands and to the specific recognition of this in the subsequent treaties. The Taipa anchorage was used greatly by foreigners because it could take larger ships than either of the Macao harbours, but the anchorage south of Coloane, in addition to its easy access to the South China Sea, is adjudged of being capable of development into a modern deep-sea port; this has introduced a new aspect to Coloane's value to Macao and to South China.

In Macao's dependencies, there are two stone memorials — one on each of the islands of Taipa and Coloane — whose stories make substantial contributions to the colony's history. But in addition to these, Coloane has a long stone story which is still yet very much in the making because from her extensive quarries she has recently supplied much of the stone needed for the causeway which now links the two islands together.

TAIPA'S MONUMENT

TAIPA'S MONUMENT tells the story of an act of revenge which was the cause of the greatest loss of life ever occasioned in the colony by a single human act. Although it had nothing directly to do with reactions to the reforms introduced by Governor Amaral, it could never have happened but for the action taken by the Portuguese government in reply to the assassination of Amaral by the Chinese.

When it was decided in Lisbon to send troops and naval vessels to Canton to avenge the Amaral outrage, the frigate *Dona Maria II* and two corvettes, the *Dom João I* and the *Iris* were dispatched with all haste to Macao, along with one of Portugal's most brilliant admirals, Pedro Alexandrino da Cunha, who was sent out as Governor with the added responsibility of directing the campaign against Canton. A detachment of Portugal's best troops arrived from Goa, but when the Admiral was able to view his task against its local background, he feared his resources were far from adequate. The situation worsened when the extra troops promised by Portugal failed to arrive (they were never sent!) and then, on 6 July 1850, hardly six weeks after Admiral Cunha's arrival in Macao, his sudden death occurred. Natural causes, and not foul play as was suspected, were established by postmortem examination to be responsible for this further blow to Macao's fortunes.

But natural causes were certainly not responsible for the setback to the Macao community which occurred about six months after Admiral Cunha's arrival and fourteen months after the death of Amaral.

On 29 October 1850, the *Dona Maria II* was lying at anchor in The Roads off Taipa in company with her two sister corvettes and the USS sloop-of-war *Marion* (566 tons and 16 guns). All the men-of-war in port were gaily bedecked with a full display of bunting in honour of the King of Portugal's birthday, and at noon their guns joined with those of the Monte Fort in booming out their congratulatory salutes. This ceremonial completed, the *Dona Maria II* was putting the last touches to her preparations to receive Macao's leading citizens on board to celebrate the royal occasion, when suddenly, at 2.30 p.m. the frigate was enveloped in a thick cloud of black smoke, and immediately the air around resounded with a thundering crash, followed by the whistling of iron and wood debris flying in all directions. When the smoke cleared, all that could be seen of the frigate was a portion of her stern fiercely burning and the sea around strewn with mangled bodies and charred wreckage. The USS *Marion* was anchored so uncomfortably close that her decks, rigging and awnings were similarly bespattered. Fortunately she was not set afire, so that the members of her crew were soon manning their boats and valiantly searching the wreckage for possible survivors. Only one of the ships complement aboard the

A MEMÓRIA DAS VICTIMAS
DA EXPLOSÃO DA FRAGATA
D. MARIA II EM 1850.
ERECTO EM 1880.

記念碑
第二瑪琍亞
戰船於己酉年轟斃者　庚辰年立

TO THE MEMORY OF THE VICTIMS
OF THE EXPLOSION ON THE FRIGATE
D. MARIA II IN 1850.
ERECTED IN 1880.

The granite monument erected on Taipa island to those who lost their lives in an explosion on board a Portuguese frigate, the Dona Maria II anchored there in 1850. The Portuguese and Chinese inscriptions, and their English translation are on the left.

Dona Maria II at the time was saved. He was a steward named Barbosa. Thirty-six other members of the crew were, luckily for them, ashore that day, or the casualty list would have been much larger. In all, 188 officers and men, including the captain, lost their lives, as well as three French prisoners and about forty Chinese who were either working on board or in junks or sampans alongside.

The cause of the disaster was said to have been a deliberate act of revenge on the part of the keeper of the ship's power-magazine. He had developed a grudge against the captain whom he believed had punished him unfairly for certain minor misdemeanours, and the keeper had also been heard to threaten to take reprisals in this way. Two other incidents have been quoted as corroborative evidence against the magazine-keeper; one was that just before the royal salute that day 'the commander had pulled him by the beard' in public for some petty irregularity; the other was that the commander's small son, a favourite with all members of the crew and especially the magazine-keeper himself, had been sent ashore for no apparent reason by the enraged keeper shortly before the disaster.

The loss of the frigate and of nearly two hundred men, and the death of Amaral's successor combined to put an end to Portugal's plans for taking armed retaliatory measures against the Chinese for Amaral's murder.

The Taipa memorial, therefore, standing just to the north of the island's police station and former fort, and overlooking the scene of the disaster it records, commemorates more than just the end of so many useful lives. It marks the abandonment of

a useless policy which would have probably caused the loss of many, many more lives than this ghastly disaster did.

Dona Maria II, after whom the ill-fated frigate was named, was the daughter of Dom Pedro, Emperor of Brazil. He became King of Portugal on the death of John VI on 10 March 1826, but he refused to leave Brazil and so he had to renounce the throne of Portugal. This he did in favour of his infant daughter, Maria da Gloria, with his brother, Dom Miguel, as Regent. Dom Miguel usurped the throne in 1828 and Maria fled to England. Pedro, however, abdicated the throne of Brazil in 1831 in order to return to Europe to reinstate his daughter, and in this, with the help of Britain, France and Spain, he was successful. Maria was restored to the throne in September 1833 and reigned as Dona Maria II until her death in 1853.

Her name is also perpetuated in Macao in connection with two other structures, both situated in the extreme north-east of the Macao peninsula. One was a fortress and the other is a road. The *Estrada de Dona Maria II* is a U-shaped road, the open end of the U facing west and embracing the *Jardim da Montanha Russa*, while its eastern bend encloses a rocky crag on which the *Fortress of Dona Maria II* was built in 1851. The fort has long since been dismantled but its site is easily identified by the masts of Macao's wireless station which now tower skywards above its shrub-covered ruins. It was one of two forts — the other is the still existing Fortress of Mong Há — both built in continuation of Amaral's plans to resist a land attack along the barrier and to give protection to those living in the area between the city walls and the barrier gate.

COLOANE'S MONUMENT

COLOANE'S MONUMENT commemorates an event which took place much more recently than any of the other events of national importance to Macao, which we have hitherto discussed. It was erected to commemorate the services to the Colony rendered by her armed forces and her police in freeing the Coloane islanders from pirate oppression as recently as 1910.

The memorial is an octagonal, truncated, slightly ornamented, obelisk standing on a small base which gives it a seemingly top heavy appearance. It is situated on the seaward side of the small public square in front of the island's chapel. To the western face of the obelisk is attached a victor's laurel wreath cast in bronze, and the front and back surfaces of the base are each inset with a marble inscription tablet. One inscription is in Portuguese and the other in Chinese, the former being on the west face, and its Portuguese inscription reads:

COMBATES
DE
COLOANE
12 e 13 DE JULHO DE
1910

The Coloane victory memorial, approximately 15 feet in height, facing west across the narrow strait that separates Coloane from the Chinese island of Wong-kam (Ilha da Montanha). Behind and separated from it by a small public square is Coloane's small chapel, built in 1934.

The operation referred to in both these inscriptions was mounted against the island stronghold of pirates operating in nearby waters. This was just another of the many periodic anti-pirate's tasks that the Portuguese inherited when they won their major pirate encounter in 1557, and Macao became theirs. It was just as imperative that the Macao forces should win this 1910 encounter, as it was in 1557, because the pirates were again not only making the surrounding seas and river estuary unsafe for peaceful and unarmed traders, but by subjugating the junk folk who fished the neighbouring waters, the pirates were gaining control of coastal communities spread over a much larger area than merely that of their island fortresses.

One particular band of pirates, led by Leung Iu Chan, and operating in the neighbourhood of Macao, established a base on Coloane at the beginning of this century, and by using the intimidating measures just mentioned, gained a hold over all the peasants and fishermen on the island.

In early July 1910, this band captured a number of children including some of wealthy Chinese merchants from a school in Chinese territory; taking them to their stronghold on Coloane, they held them there to ransom for a sum which constituted a large amount of money at that time. The Macao authorities failed in their official attempts to make contact with the pirates and when a small force of police were sent to rescue the children and encountered strong resistance, it was realized that the police had a task of no small magnitude on their hands.

The party of police, having suffered a number of casualties including one dead, were withdrawn and plans were drawn up to mount an operation of a size commensurate with the need to free the whole island from pirate influence as well as to rescue the children. The Macao military forces were mobilized and what naval craft were available, patrolled the waters around the island to prevent any of the pirates from escaping. China too held a number of her gunboats in readiness outside Macao waters to help if needed.

After a preliminary bombardment of the pirate positions by the Portuguese gunboats, a combined force of military and police landed on Coloane on the night of 11 July. On the following days, a number of fierce but scattered encounters took place on the island, and eventually the pirates, with the exception of a few who made good their escape from the island, were subdued, their strongholds destroyed and the children hostages freed. The killed and wounded among the pirates were reported to number over 150, and those captured, who numbered more than 50, were all tried in the Macao courts.

Although it cannot be claimed that this armed action eradicated piracy completely from the waters of the Canton river estuary and of the Ladrones, it did establish once and for all complete Portuguese jurisdiction in fact as well as on paper, over both Macao's island dependencies of Taipa and Coloane.

Coloane has ever since celebrated its complete freedom thus gained, by recognizing 13 July every year to be a public holiday throughout the island.

Such are some of the voices which speak from Taipa and Coloane stones, but these were not the only islands which the Macao authorities at various times have looked upon as being among their dependencies. Some writers have even claimed that the whole of the island of Heung Shan was included in the original understanding between the Chinese and the Portuguese; but in these days most people would regard this claim as more in the nature of wishful thinking. But there is no doubt that the

Portuguese looked upon Lappa Island immediately west of Macao, Pac-Sa-Lan opposite Taipa and Ilha da Montanha west of Coloane, as theirs. To the island of Pac-Sa-Lan, we shall have occasion to refer later because the Macao government built the leprosarium there in 1852, where it remained until it was transferred to Coloane in 1965.

BARRIERS AND PORTALS

IT IS DIFFICULT at this point in time to decide whether the first barrier set up by the Chinese to separate off the Macao peninsula from the rest of the island of Heung Shan, was built along a previously agreed international line or whether its line was chosen for reasons of expediency and was subsequently adopted as the international boundary. Probably the latter is the more likely, for in those days such a barrier was built primarily for protection and secondly to facilitate the control of traffic in both people and produce across its line. However, much of the peninsula the Chinese envisaged as having been transferred to the Portuguese, the isthmus was the natural place for them to build their barrier; it followed the shortest line across the peninsula and was therefore the cheapest to build and the easiest to control and to defend. Its actual length was approximately 1500 feet and in each foot was vested the same responsibility as its counterpart — the Great Wall of China — placed in each mile of its long stretch from the Yellow Sea to Chinwangtao. The responsibility of the northern wall was to protect the heart of the Kingdom from being overrun by barbarians from northern neighbouring states, while the southern wall was to prevent penetration of China's territory and contamination of its people by oversea barbarians from Europe's maritime countries.

It is not without significance that whereas European settlers in other parts of the globe almost invariably surrounded their settlements with stockades or fortified walls, it was the Chinese who built the first barrier between themselves and the Macao Portuguese. This was in 1573 and it followed almost exactly the line of the present wall which is regarded now as the international boundary, and its gate was in the same position as the present Barrier Gate. The first gate, with its motto warning all those who could read Chinese to 'Dread our greatness and respect our virtue', survived until the Passaleão incident two and three-quarter centuries later, and during that period it was the only overland means of access recognized officially by the Chinese as a portal of entry to their country. All overseas foreigners therefore who wished to obtain official permission to enter China, be they merchants or missionaries, envoys of sovereign states or representatives from vassal peoples, all came first to Macao where the barrier and its gate were the symbols which indicated they must there await official sanction to proceed further. On receiving this, they either passed through this gate or were forced by it and the barrier to use river channels to Canton. Thus, from 1573 until the opening of the Treaty Ports after the first Sino-British War, the gate was the Barrier Gate for local use and Macao itself was the Barrier Gate to the Middle Kingdom for the whole of the overseas world.

For many years the *Portas do Cerco* remained a closed area where photography was forbidden. The area around the Barrier Gate was renovated in 1994 and inaugurated by the Governor of Macao, General Vasco Rocha Viera on 12 January 1994. A walkway has been constructed to the old Barrier Gate, whilst new exit points from Macao and entry points into

A POLÍCIA DE SEGURANÇA
PÚBLICA HERDEIRA DE UM
PASSADO CUJA ORIGEM
REMONTA À CRIAÇÃO DE
MACAU, COMEMORA PELA,
VEZ PRIMEIRA O DIA DA
POLÍCIA NA DATA DA
ASSINATURA EM 14 MAR
1691 DO ALVARÁ RÉGIO
QUE CONFIRMA A
NOMEAÇÃO JÁ ANTIGA
PELO LEAL SENADO DOS
CAPITÃES DA GENTE DO
ORDENANÇA.

MACAU. 14 MAR 1984.

*New tablet referring to old stones with inscriptions in Portuguese believed to have been incorporated
in the original gate on the wall separating Macao from China, and said to have been saved and
preserved by the Senate when the first gate was destroyed after the Passaleão incident.*

Gongbei have been constructed on either side. It is now possible to walk all the way to the barrier gate, the entrance to which has been sealed with glass. On the other side, the banyan trees which once led into the paddy fields now straggle towards the new Chinese Customs post. The walk to the barrier gate comprises 16 *azulejos*, including scenes from Macao's recent history. The drawing of the city of Macao by the English visitor Peter Mundy is reproduced, as are a number of both European and Chinese maps of Macao and several street scenes.

The early barrier gate is commemorated in a stone in the left-hand wall of the Barrier Gate.

Only two stones of this gate are known to still exist. They are embedded in the northern wall of the entrance hall of the Leal Senado, one being inscribed BOUNDARY GATE in Portuguese, and the other CUSTOMS GATE in Chinese. They are believed in some quarters to have been carved and placed in the Gate by orders of Governor Amaral, but with the enmity existing between the two countries during his governorship, this seems highly unlikely. It is quite possible that the one in Portuguese was put up by Amaral but it is more likely that the other was carved by the Chinese, for they do indicate the manner in which the two peoples formerly regarded the structure, the Portuguese as a warning to their people that they had reached the limit of their territory, while the Chinese looked upon it as a place for collecting customs fees.

The present wall, built by the Portuguese after

64

Mesquita's victory at Passaleão, was a barrier against further possible overland threats to their territory, and the present gate was built in 1870, appropriately resembling a triumphal arch. Above the arch is carved a quotation from the works of Camoens — A PÁTRIA HONRAI QUE A PÁTRIA VOS CONTEMPLA (Honour your country and your country will have regard for you) — below which are carved emblems of Portugal's armed forces together with the dates of Amaral's assassination (22 de Agosto de 1849) and of Mesquita's victory at Passaleão (25 de Agosto de 1849). The date of the commencement of the construction of the gate (22 de Agosto de 1870) and of its completion or of its opening (31 de Outubro 1871) are carved inside the arch. None of these adornments could be examined closely, as only officials on duty and peasants bringing their produce from nearby extramural fields for sale in Macao's markets were permitted access to the gate, under orders strictly enforced by both Chinese and Portuguese armed guards.

For some decades after the Chinese built their first barrier, the Portuguese were content to allow the Chinese to control the number of their nationals passing to and fro; but the number coming in with the intention of obtaining employment and settling in the city increased until it was feared that their numbers might constitute an internal threat to the community's security. Strong points surrounded by protective walls were built by the Portuguese, but the Chinese frowned on these evidences of a developing system of fortification.

After the abortive Dutch invasion of 1622, the justification for such defence works against a possible sea attack was established, and the fears of the Chinese that fortifications were directed against them were allayed sufficiently to allow the

A portion of the Macao city wall built in the 1660s on Guia Hill near the present hospital of S. Januário. This fragment demonstrates how resistant its material is to Macao's extremes of climate and rainfall.

Portuguese to build a strong city wall around the settlement. It ran from the fortress of S. Francisco in the east via the Monte Fort to the Inner Harbour in the north-west. Ingress or egress to and from the city was possible at two points only, the Gate of St. Anthony near the present church of that name, and the Campo Gate near the present Rua do Campo. These gates were closed each night and all Chinese had to leave the city before dusk and return to their villages in the area between the city gates and the barrier. The city wall and its gates stood until the 1860s when they were demolished. Only isolated fragments of the wall still exist and from these it is possible to establish with accuracy both its position and composition. It was made of rammed earth, known locally as 'chunam'. The demolition of this city wall and the removal of its gates made it possible for the city to expand into the Campo, and by taking advantage of Governor Amaral's plans of twenty years earlier, to develop into the extensive city we know today.

The Cathedral of Macao by George Smirnoff

View of the fortress and lighthouse of Guia by George Smirnoff

View of the small chapel of São Tiago da Barra, with the walls of the old fortress behind it, painted by George Smirnoff in 1945

Watercolour by George Smirnoff, detailing the old fortress of Dona Maria II as it appeared in 1945. The large banyan tree, painted then, is still there today.

View of St. Paul's Collegiate Church, seen from the ramparts of The Monte, by George Smirnoff

View of the fountain in the São Francisco Gardens, painted by George Smirnoff in 1945

Flora Gardens by Vicente Pacia

The bust of Luís de Camões (Camoens) found in the Grotto of Camoens, by George Smirnoff

Stones, Ecclesiastical and Secular

IN THE HISTORY of the Province of Macao there are many milestones, the consideration of which lead to a clearer understanding of the stages of its development over the last four centuries. Some of these milestones are personal memorials, others are buildings — many still in use, but some alas, in ruins — and a few now exist only in Macao's archives. We start our consideration of these historical milestones with a study of one which is of fundamental ecclesiastical interest.

THE CATHEDRAL OF MACAO AND THE CHURCH OF ST. LAZARUS

MACAO, THE TRADING POST, was first settled by Portuguese merchant adventurers from Malacca; similarly, as a centre of organized Christian endeavour, Macao arose as an extension of the Diocese of Malacca which was instituted as early as 4 February 1558. From that year until 1562, under the authority of the *Padroado* (the Patronage of the Holy See whereby Portugal acquired the sole right of administering all the affairs of the church between the Cape of Good Hope and Japan), ecclesiastical Macao was administered indirectly from distant Goa through the Bishop of Malacca as a part of his diocese. When he moved to Malacca in 1562 to take up his residence in his diocese, he immediately sent a secular priest to Macao, appointing him Vicar of the principal church in the settlement. He was Father João Soares, and he arrived in Macao either towards the end of 1562 or at the beginning of 1563, and forthwith took over the Church of Our Lady of Hope (later known as the Church of St. Lazarus) which had been founded four years earlier in 1558.

Ecclesiastical Macao continued to be administered from 1563 by the Bishop of Malacca's resident representative until 1568 when the Church in Macao was divorced from the Diocese of Malacca and its administration transferred to a special Vatican representative as a prelude to the eventual establishment of Macao's own diocese with its own Bishop. The new appointee was Dom Melchior Carneiro, SJ, who had become but a few years previously, titular Bishop of Nicaea and Coadjutor to the Patriarch of Ethiopia, with the special assignment of establishing a *rapproachement* between the Ethiopian Church and the Church of Rome. He sailed from Europe to Goa, intending to approach north Africa from India, but the political situation in Ethiopia at the time made it inadvisable for him to attempt to enter that country. He did not return to Europe forthwith, but remained in Goa awaiting instructions from Rome. These eventually arrived, appointing him Apostolic Administrator of Far Eastern Missions with the same patriarchal status as he had previously been given. Dom Melchior unfortunately was an asthmatic, and so when he found that the climate of Goa did not suit him, he moved his residence to Malacca which had the reputation of being healthier than Goa. This turned out to be an advantageous move for shortly after his arrival in Malacca, he received his appointment from the Pope as Administrator Apostolic to Macao, the Diocese of Macao being eventually created by the Bull of Pope Gregory XIII (*Super Specular Militantis Ecclesiae*) dated 23 January 1575. But, as Father Teixeira has pointed out, this date, traditionally celebrated as the anniversary of the founding of the diocese, does not take into account the date changes consequent upon the adoption in 1582 of the Gregorian, in place of the Julian, calendar. Father Teixeira therefore rightly claims that for anniversary purposes, the year of the founding of the diocese should be considered to be 1576. The new diocese had ecclesiastical jurisdiction over 'Macao, China and Japan, and all the islands adjacent thereto', the bishop being styled as the 'Bishop of China and Japan in Macao'. It was not until 1623 that the first Macao cathedral, built on the present site in *Largo de Sé*, was opened, and until that date the Church of Our Lady of Hope,

enjoyed the status of *primus inter pares* among Macao's churches. This status, earned four centuries ago and enjoyed for only five decades, is relived for a brief hour whenever a new bishop is appointed. On his arrival in Macao, his first official act is to visit the Church of Our Lady of Hope where he is welcomed to his See, after which a procession leads him to the Cathedral for the public proclamation of the Papal Bull appointing him Bishop of the Diocese and for his enthronement. Apart from this participation in the preliminaries to the enthronement ceremonies of a new bishop, the only other reminder of the former status of the Church of Our Lady of Hope (St. Lazarus), is that it has remained an official parish church. In all other ways, it is just one of the many churches of the diocese.

It has long been the custom in Portugal to erect a large cross outside, and in close proximity to, each of its churches. This tradition has been faithfully followed in Macao ever since the foundation of the settlement. In this case, the cross stands facing north-west in the southern corner of the courtyard in front of the church, and the name *CRUX DA ESPERANÇA* (The Cross of Hope) is a reminder that the real name of the church is the CHURCH OF OUR LADY OF HOPE, and according to tradition it was originally built for the lepers who lived in a small village of their own just outside one of the city gates that was not far from where the Church of St. Anthony now stands. In this village, Macao's first bishop, Dom Melchior Carneiro, founded a hospice for lepers in association with the *Santa Casa da Misericordia*, and it was not long before common custom and usage attached the name *São Lázaro*, to all these new entities, the village, the church, the hospice and the city gate. The village and the city gate have long since

Left: The cross at the Church of St. Lazarus. *Above:* The Latin inscription on the north-west face of the very substantial base of the cross, in which Portuguese spelling is used in the date (vide ANO 1637).

disappeared, but the hospice and the church still exist, in other forms and other places, and the church is still commonly known as the Church of St. Lazarus. The significance of the date 1637 on its cross is explained in the upper of the two inscriptions to be seen on commemorative stones on the south side of the main door of the church nearby. These inscriptions refer to the earlier churches which formerly occupied the site. The lower inscription is in Portuguese; it refers to the present church, while the upper is in Latin and its gilded lettering is cut on a marble slab attached to the church wall.

The following is the English translation of the inscription:

Upper
TO THE MOST GOOD AND THE MOST GREAT GOD THIS TEMPLE

Lower
PUBLIC WORKS OF MACAO.
CONSTRUCTED BY ORDER OF
HIS EXCELLENCY THE GOVERNOR
THOMAZ DE SOUZA ROZA
1885–1886

Photographs of inscriptions on the south side of the main door of the
Church of St. Lazarus. **Above:** The upper inscription in Latin.
Below: The lower inscription is cut on a granite stone in Portuguese.

The governor who is mentioned in the lower of these two inscriptions is remembered by Macao, not so much for his part in the rebuilding of one of its churches, as for his services during the final stages in 1886 of Macao's long struggle for recognition by China of her colony status. It was Governor de Souza Roza who went to Peking on this mission and it was he who secured the written and signed agreement on which Portugal's claim to Macao's national status now rests.

Soon after its foundation, the new diocese of Macao was confronted with problems which arose directly out of the Atlantic Demarcation Line agreed upon by Spain and Portugal in the fifteenth century. Portugal explored and developed its area east of that Line until it embraced India, Malaya, China and Japan and the ecclesiastical administration of these latter two areas devolved upon Macao's diocese. This is reflected in the original official title of the Bishop. But the Spanish, when they became established in the Philippines, refused to acknowledge this evangelistic monopoly claimed by Portugal. We shall discuss later the effects of the work of the Spanish in Japan and their attempts to infiltrate into China even by way of Macao itself but here we confine our attention to the achievements of the Portuguese priests in China and Japan. They were mainly Jesuits, specially trained in the Jesuit foundations in Macao for this work. These were St. Paul's Church and College for priests for Japan and the Seminary of St. Joseph founded in 1728 for the training of Jesuit priests for China. All Jesuit lines of communication from Japan and China therefore led back to Macao, and this explains why all the changes in China and Japan, political and mercantile as well as ecclesiastical, were reflected in the history of the church and state in Macao.

When, for instance, the church in Japan became a separate diocese in 1588, Macao retained the responsibility for only China, Cochin China, Korea and for the neighbouring islands as far off shore as Formosa and Hainan. This necessitated the change in the Macao Bishop's title from Bishop of Japan and China, in use from 1576, to Bishop of China. This title remained in use until 1690 by which time, in spite of difficulties and reverses, the Roman Catholic Church in China prospered to such an extent that further administrative decentralization from Macao became essential. In 1658, Tonking was separated off under a Vicar Apostolic and this appointment was closely followed by others in Cochin-China and in China itself. On 10 April 1690, Pope Alexander VIII founded, under the *Padroado*, the separate dioceses of Peking and Nanking, and so with independent Apostolic Prefectures being set up in south-east and in south-west China under *Propaganda Fide*, the Bishop of Macao was left from 1690 onwards with the responsibility of the administration of only the colony itself, plus Hainan and 'The Two Kwangs'. Of these portions of China remaining under Macao's ecclesiastic jurisdiction, Kwangsi and Kwangtung gradually became almost exclusively a French missionary area and in 1850, it too became an Apostolic Prefecture, independent of Macao.

In Macao itself, church administration also underwent a number of significant changes. Of its early churches, only three were parish churches. They were the churches of St. Lazarus (Our Lady of Hope), St. Lawrence and St. Anthony. When the Cathedral was built, it became the fourth parish church, but it was not until this century that a fifth was added — the Taipa church. As recently as 1966, the Church of Our Lady of Fatima was built in the overcrowded refugee border-area of Macao, and it became the province's sixth parish church. But an internal development that was of just as great a significance to her neighbours, future as well as contemporary, as it was to Macao itself, was the arrival there of Procurators of the Congregation for the Propagation of Faith. This is the supreme body in Rome responsible for the planning and execution of the missionary policy of the Catholic Church. Its area of operation was worldwide, only the Portuguese mission areas being excluded. Under the *Padroado*, the missionary work of the Catholic Church in China, especially that based on Macao, was already provided for; it was a Portuguese responsibility in an exclusively Portuguese domain. The establishment in Macao of this Congregation from Rome was therefore strongly resented by the Portuguese, the more so since the Procurators were all Italians. It is not possible to say how far this local antagonism influenced Mgr Jovanni Baptista Marchini when he was in charge of the office, to move it to Canton, but he was soon expelled from there by the Chinese and had to return to Macao, where he died in 1823. Mgr Marchini was buried in the Church of St. Joseph's Seminary, his memorial there taking the form of a marble facing on the pillar to the left of the chancel of the Church. It bears an indistinct Latin inscription, an English translation of which reads:

JOVANNI BAPTISTA MARCHINI, A NATIVE OF TORTONA, PROTONOTARY APOSTOLIC, PROCURATOR OF THE CONGREGATION FOR THE PROPAGATION OF THE FAITH, RENOWNED FOR HIS PIETY, LEARNING AND HIS COUNSEL CONCERNING CHRISTIAN DOCTRINE. FOR HIS SERVICES TO THE SPREADING OF CHRISTIANITY AMONG THE CHINESE HIS FELLOW ITALIAN, CAROLUS VIDUA

CONZANI, CAUSED THIS MEMORIAL TO BE PLACED HERE. HE LIVED TO BE 65 YEARS OF AGE AND DIED IN MACAO IN THE YEAR 1823.

This setback in Canton for the *Propaganda Fide* was only temporary however, for with the founding of a settlement by the British on the north shore of the island of Hong Kong on 26 January 1841, a totally new religious requirement in south China immediately arose. It was that of supplying the parish needs to Europeans of the Roman Catholic faith who had settled on a barren and almost uninhabited island, a mile or so off the China coast. Whose duty was this? Was it the responsibility of the Bishop of Macao, under the *Padroado*, or was it the responsibility of the representative of the Congregation for the Propagation of the Faith? The problem was solved by action, not deliberation. The representative of the *Propaganda Fide* in Macao at that time was a young and energetic priest, Father Theodore Joset, and he immediately recommended to Rome the establishment of a mission in Hong Kong. The Vatican approved and, by Papal decree, on 22 April 1841,

Hong Kong and an area of six leagues around it was formed into a new ecclesiastical Prefecture, with Father, now Mgr Joset in charge.

Mgr Joset's first action was to visit Hong Kong, secure a piece of land and set up a matshed church. The site chosen was on the high ground where Wellington and Pottinger Streets now meet, and there he subsequently also provided accommodation for his office of Propagation of the Faith — which he later transferred permanently from Macao — and for an extension of his Macao seminary for the trading of Chinese priests. Here is further evidence, in this case ecclesiastic and academic, of Macao's cradling of Hong Kong, and it would be interesting to know how far Mgr Joset's foresight was due to his confidence in a British Hong Kong or to his desire at all costs to escape from the difficulties, personal and institutional, arising out of the presence of his office in Macao. Certainly, he had nothing to lose by the move for even if Hong Kong was a failure, he could always go back to Macao as Father Marchini had done from Canton.

Mgr Joset died in Hong Kong in August 1842 and, as the founder of the Roman Catholic Church in Hong Kong, his mortal remains were accorded a fitting resting place behind the high altar in the Catholic Cathedral which was subsequently built above Caine Road. His successor was Mgr Feliciani, an Italian Franciscan, who in turn was followed in 1855 by Fr Aloysius Ambrosi. By their combined efforts, these two Italian priests arranged for the Institute of Foreign Missions of Milan — which in 1926 became the Pontifical Institute, *Pontificio Instituto dei Missioni Estere* — to assume the responsibility of staffing the mission in Hong Kong as a Prefecture Apostolic, later to become a Diocese. This explains why, in spite of the presence in the neighbourhood, of Portuguese secular priests and members of religious orders, the Roman Catholic Church in Hong Kong became an Italian mission and subsequently an Italian bishopric.

CHURCHES AND FORTRESSES

THE CONSIDERATION OF churches and fortresses under one heading is not as incongruous as it may at first sight appear. It had long been the custom in Europe for convents and monasteries to surround themselves by substantial walls, primarily for seclusion from the prying eyes of the outside world, and only secondarily for protection, and never as a base for offence. In isolated places like Macao, protection probably assumed a relatively greater importance as is shown by the fact that in some cases the convent wall was joined to the larger system of protective city walls, for instance, at the Franciscan and Jesuit enclaves. It is not surprising therefore that the Chinese looked upon both fortresses and churches with suspicion, for they could not be expected to distinguish between the defensive walls of the latter and the offensive bulwarks of the former. Only distance from China's boundary rendered a walled area free from suspicion of being a potential offensive base. There is at least one case on record of mandarin officials being invited to inspect monastic walls before they could be convinced of their peaceful role.

Macao's earliest churches and hermitages were built by priests and members of the Monastic Orders to meet the spiritual needs of the earliest traders whom they accompanied on their explorations. Small chapels too were erected in the various fortresses that were built for the protection of the young settlement. The most likely source of attack in those days was from the sea, either by Chinese or Japanese pirates or by Western maritime rivals. Nevertheless, the possibility of an overland attack from China could not altogether be ignored by the Portuguese, and the Chinese were conscious of this suspicion for the mandarins were quick to indicate that they would look upon it as an hostile act if land defences of any kind were erected anywhere near their border. Six military forts well outside the Chinese suspicion zone were early planned by the Portuguese. Three of these were built on headlands for coastal defence — S. Francisco, Bomparto and Barra — and three for inland defence on the settlement's highest hills — Guia, The Monte and Penha. Extensive fortifications were constructed at Guia or The Monte, but Penha remained a small hermitage chapel, walled and with a commanding view, but otherwise unfortified. They each had their chapel, for example: *Nossa Senhora de S. Paulo do Monte* (Our Lady of the Mount of St. Paul); *Nossa Senhora da Guia* (Our Lady of Guia); *S. Tiago da Barra* (St. James of the Barra), and *Nossa Senhora de Bomparto* (Our Lady of Good Delivery).

These fortress chapels were intended mainly for the use of the fort personnel, and were therefore small in size and simple in design. They were, however, open to the public for devotional exercises on special occasions such as the Feast Day of each chapel's patron saint, and some are still thus used by members of the civil community. As the security of the settlement became more assured, the building of new churches and the replacement of some of the earlier temporary ones by more permanent buildings followed. Three of these early houses were set up by members of Spanish Orders.

A comprehensive history of all Macao's churches lies outside the scope of this work and the same may be said of full histories of its major forts. But some of the chapels within the forts, as well as some of the forts themselves, shelter stones which are so intimately interwoven with important events in Macao's early history that although their detailed consideration fits in better under other headings in these records, general reference is made to many of them here for the sake of convenience.

THE MONTE FORTRESS

The Monte Fort is a case in point. It is one of Macao's most important historic monuments and a visitor is forcibly reminded of this by the arrestingly worded inscription on the bronze place attached to the outside of the south wall, immediately to the west of the fort's only entrance.

HALT! ATTENTION! RECALL FOR A FEW MOMENTS THE BEAUTIFUL HISTORY OF OUR COUNTRY. ENTER WITH PRIDE AND WITH HEAD ERECT IF YOU ARE A SOLDIER OF THIS COUNTRY.

Left: The Portuguese inscription cast in bronze and attached to the south wall near the entrance of the Monte Fort. Right: An English translation of the inscription.

A gate guards this entrance which, via a short passage through the wall, opens onto a narrow ramp which leads by means of two right-angled turns, to the grassed fortress-square above. Built into the west wall of this passage and facing the visitor at the first turn of the ramp, is a granite memorial dated 1626. The memorial is composed of four separate pieces of granite, an upper one in the shape of an isosceles triangle resting on the other three to give an overall height of 6 feet to the *ensemble*. Of the lower three stones, the central one is rectangular in shape (32 inches wide by 38 inches in height) and it is flanked on either side by two slender cylindrical columns, 4 inches in diameter and 38 inches high. A carving occupies the plane surface of the lower rectangular stone, plus that of the inner part (24 inches high) of the upper triangular stone. The equal sides of the latter project above the carved surface form a gable-shaped canopy for the whole memorial. The commemorative stone is set into the wall of the approach to the square inside the Monte Fort. Its height, measured from its base to the top of the carved device on the ridge of the gable is 6 feet, and its width between the lateral columns is 3 feet 4 inches and that between the projecting eaves of the gable is 4 feet.

The lower portion of the carving depicts the Portuguese coat of arms, the shield being flanked on either side by a smiling unadorned angel, one supporting above his head an armillary sphere and the other the equi-limbed cross of Portugal. Below the coat of arms is carved a date, the word DOMINI being contracted to DNI, and the dots over the I and the figure 1 in the date of the year 1626, as well as the punctuation full stops, being represented by small crosses. Under the gable on the surface of the upper triangular stone, the bust of St. Paul, haloed

and with a drawn sword resting on his right shoulder, is depicted in semi-relief. This religious theme, plus the use of the crosses as punctuations marks, favours the religious origin of the stone and of the Fort; the date carved on it, AD 1626, indicates that it is not a foundation stone, but commemorates the completion of the fortress in that year. Its construction was undoubtedly begun by the Jesuits, but historians are still unable to agree upon an exact date. It was certainly considerably earlier than 1626 for by 1622 the building of the fortress was already well enough advanced for one gun at least to be used against the invading Dutch forces. The Jesuits, however, built only three of the bastions, a fourth being added between 1622 and 1626 by the military authorities according to the plans originally drawn up as early as 1626 by Francisco Lopes Carrasco. The completed fortress consisted eventually therefore of four bastions, one at each corner of an almost right-angled parallelogram formed by four high, castellated walls. The whole of the enclosed area was raised to within but a few feet of the level of the battlemented parapet, thus forming the fortress-square. The parapets were pierced at regular intervals by embrasures, wide enough to mount guns. Several of these embrasures still house guns but they are merely showpieces of the 1860 period. The early historical importance of The Monte — the abbreviated title by which the fortress is familiarly known — lies in the relations it reveals between church and state, which were sometimes friendly, but at other times markedly antagonistic. The site on which the fort was built was a part of a much larger site originally allotted to the Jesuits. The full site included that on which the Collegiate Church of St. Paul stood, now the enclosure behind its ruined façade; the area covered by the imposing flight of granite steps leading up to the façade; the area immediately on the right as one approaches the bottom of this flight of steps, originally occupied by the College of St. Paul and now covered by a block of houses; and a substantial area just to the south of the College site which has recently been reacquired by the Jesuits, and on which they have built the *Instituto Dom Melchior Carneiro, SJ.*

Following the custom referred to above, the Jesuits surrounded all this property with a high thick wall, and by linking it up with the city wall and making it of the same 'chunam' material, it aroused but little suspicion among the mandarin officials. For the defence of their property, the Jesuits naturally chose the neighbouring mount as a site for a battery. When therefore in 1615, the King of Spain — who was then also King of Portugal — issued instructions for the fortifying of Macao against a possible attack by the Dutch, it suited the Macao civil officials to persuade the Jesuits to fortify the mount for their own and incidentally for the community's defence. This seems the most likely and reasonable explanation of the many variants of the story as to how the Jesuits came to build the Monte Fort, and it also explains the inclusion of the new fortress within the wall system which the Jesuits had already built around their College and Church property. This was accomplished by building two other walls, one connecting that at present forming the northern boundary of the Dom Melchior Carneiro Institute, to the south-east bastion of the fort, and the other from the south-west bastion to the former Collegiate Church of St. Paul. In the base of the wall between these two bastions, an underground entrance to the fort was made, evidence of which is still visible from the Institute below. The Jesuits also used this

entrance to the fort in 1622 when nuns and priests were evacuated to the safety of The Monte from the Franciscan convent during the Dutch bombardment prior to their landing at Caçilhas Bay.

After the victory over the Dutch, the Jesuits continued building the fort, but in 1623 an important change was made in the government of Macao. It ceased to be governed by an annually appointed Captain-Major of the Japan Voyage, the appointment being changed to a three-year one to the dual post of Governor and Captain-General. The first appointee was chosen, be it noted, by the inhabitants of Macao. He was Dom Francisco Mascarenhas and he held the dual post from 1623–1626, but from the outset the new appointment was an unhappy one. The people of Macao had not realized what increased powers the Governor had been given but they soon did so when he began to exercise them immediately after his arrival. He did not conceal his displeasure at being accommodated in an ordinary house instead of in a palace, and he forthwith began to look with covetous eyes on the Jesuit's citadel on the mount. The Jesuits saw in him a threat to their already established supremacy in local affairs, while the people openly ignored him especially when he issued orders 'in the name of the King'. Feelings between the Governor on the one hand and the people and the Jesuits on the other reached such a height that the Governor's unpopularity forced him to seek refuge in the Convent of St. Augustine; but even there he was not completely safe from the guns of the fort which crashed three cannon balls through the walls of the convent.

But Dom Francisco Mascarenhas won out in the end. On indicating his desire to visit the Monte Fort and see the unsurpassed view of his colony from the battlements, he was invited by the Jesuits to do so. To pay his hosts the greater honour, he was accompanied by a larger retinue than usual, most of whom were his bodyguard in mufti. The party was a great success but eventually the Jesuits had to break the news to their guest, as gently as possible, that the time for closing the gate was approaching. To this His Excellency replied with complete composure that they need not worry about that, for the gate had already been closed by his men, and would be opened on the morrow 'in the King's name'. In the meantime, the Jesuits were ignominiously forced out of the fort through a small passage leading to their convent below. The exit was immediately closed and sealed, and whether the story concerning the use to which the passage was put is apocryphal or not, proof of its earlier existence has been established by the recent discovery of a blocked-up entrance to the fort in the base of its western wall.

Following the seizure of the fort by Dom Francisco Mascarenhas, he completed the building, at the same time adding to the plans, barracks for the soldiers and a residence of considerable size for himself. In this way therefore, although the major part of the fort was built by Jesuit priests (some even assisting in the manual labour itself) and at the expense of their own Society, it eventually became the keystone of Portugal's plan for the defence of Macao. Succeeding governors completed the remainder of the royal plan by strengthening or building the additional forts or shore batteries of S. Francisco, Guia, Bomparto and of S. Tiago da Barra, but they would all have been of little value were it not for the local availability supplies of copper tin and the genius of Manoel Tavares Bocarro (1625–1675), an expert in the art of bronze casting.

He set up his foundry on the shore level just east of the Bomparto fort now known as Rua do Chunambeiro, which is situated at the western end of the Praia Grande. This foundry became the most famous in the Far East for casting cannon and bells, and for more than twenty years, it supplied these to forts, churches and ships as far north as Manchuria and Japan, and as far south as Malacca. Besides rendering this valuable commercial service to Macao, Bocarro served its community as Governor from 1657–1664. In recent years, the buildings on the north-western and north-eastern sides of the fortress-square have housed Macao's metereological station.

The building housing the meteriological station was demolished in 1996. In its place the Museu de Macau has been built, with an approach set into the western wall of The Monte. The Museu de Macau combines well-thought-out contents and excellent design, and is an excellent addition to Macao's collection of museums.

GUIA FORTRESS

THE GUIA HILL IS the only one of Macao's early fortifications to be built outside the city or without any continuity between its walls and those of the city itself such as we have seen to occur in the case of The Monte. In addition to the Dutch prisoners which it housed in person and in stone it still houses two historical stones of general Macao interest. One is a commemorative stone on the outside of the fortress wall, and the other a memorial stone in its small chapel.

The Guia hill has always been considered of strategic importance in any plan for the defence of the Macao peninsula and mention of a Guia Fort

77

figures in the reports of its defence against the Dutch in 1622. The present fort, built in 1637–1638, cannot therefore be the first to occupy this site. Nor is its chapel the first Chapel of Our Lady of Guia, for in 1633, when a party of nuns, the Poor Clares, arrived from Manila to found a convert in Macao, they were reported as being housed temporarily in the Chapel of Our Lady of Guia, until their own accommodation (later occupied by the Franciscan Missionaries of Mary) was ready for them. The present chapel is inside the fort, and on one of its paving stones just inside the door is the inscription pictured and described below.

*The granite commemorative stone, 2 feet 9 inches wide and 2 feet 3 inches high at its highest point, set at a height of about 10 feet from the ground in the north-west face of the outside wall near the entrance to the Guia Fort. The inscription is carved in Portuguese without any spacing between the words, or any punctuation marks to indicate abbreviations or the end of a sentence. Carved in low relief above the lettering is the shield of Portugal's coat of arms, flanked on one side by the armillary sphere, and on the other by a cross **patte**.*

ESTE FORTE MANDOV FAZER A CIDADE A SVA / CVSTA PELO CAPITAO DARTILHARIA ANT. RIBR. / RAIA. COMESOV-SE EN SETEBRO DE 1637 ACABOV-SE / EN MARCO D 1638 SENDO GERAL DA CAMARA / DE NORONHA.

THE CITY ORDERED THIS FORT TO BE BUILT AT ITS OWN EXPENSE BY CAPTAIN OF THE ARTILLERY, ANTONIO RIBEIRO RAIA. IT WAS STARTED IN SEPTEMBER 1637 AND WAS FINISHED IN MARCH 1638, THE GENERAL THEN BEING DA CAMARA DE NORONHA.

The inscription in Portuguese and its English translation reproduced with normal spacing and punctuation marks added. Ends of lines are indicated by oblique strokes.

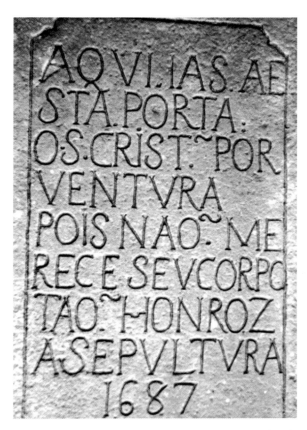

A QUI IAS A ESTA PORTA: OS CRIST. POR
VENTURA POIS NAO. MERECE SEU CORPO TAO.
HONROZA SEPULTURA 1687

HERE AT THIS DOOR LIES THE SEXTON
WHOSE BODY ONLY BY CHANCE MERITS
SUCH AN HONOURABLE BURIAL 1687

The Portuguese inscription, with abbreviations, set out with the customary spacing between the words. An English translation of the inscription is shown below it.

The inscription on the upper half of a paving-stone memorial in the Guia Chapel. The complete stone measures 6 feet 6 inches by 2 feet 6 inches.

The lower portion of the stone depicted in the above photograph shows the large space left between the main part of the inscription and the single line at the bottom of the stone (in which the Ns are carved in reverse).

The inscription is well preserved in spite of the wear and tear of over two and a half centuries of foot traffic to which it has been exposed. It is also well carved and is in a style typical of the late seventeenth century; it uses large letters and frequent abbreviations, and its lines are all of equal length occupying the full width of the space available within a simple, thin-lined border. In addition, the line at the bottom of the stone — 1720 ANNOS — contains an excellent example of space-saving of the period; the terminal S of ANNOS is carved within the circle of the preceding letter O, producing the composite letter-compounds. It is difficult to explain the need for this space-saving, because a gap of 2 feet 2 inches had already been left between this line and the date 1687 in the main inscription above. Obviously, this space was intended for some other use, such as for other members of the sexton's family whom he may have predeceased. It could be that the whole inscription as it now reads was cut in 1720, in which case it was not composed by the sexton himself but by friends who knew by what 'chance' he came to be buried at the entrance to the Chapel, for there were, and still are, preferences and priorities to be considered in allotting burial sites within churches and church precincts. Apparently, this humble sexton could never normally have aspired to such an honourable status and it was only 'by chance' that he achieved it. As yet we have no information as to how this fortuitous chance came his way. It is difficult to imagine the ordinary duties of a seventeenth-century sexton providing the opportunity for a service so notable as to merit such recognition, unless his duties also included some public service in which exceptional devotion to duty might well come to the notice of high officials.

It so happens that his normal duties did include such an extra service — that of notifying the Macao community of the approach of ships to the colony, the direction of their approach, and their nature, whether merchantmen, men-of-war or pirates. The lookout was in Guia Fort and the sexton broadcast his announcements to the public by means of a bell. The last bell to be used for this purpose is in a wooden belfry which is about 6 feet high and mounted outside the chapel immediately to the north of its entrance; it was cast in 1707 and was recast in 1824. No information is available concerning the bell which existed when the sexton who is buried in the chapel was responsible for the lookout. The history of the present bell is briefly related in two announcements, the individual letters of which are cast separately and affixed to the side of the bell, one on the side next to the chapel wall and the other on the south-west aspect of the bell.

PENHA

THE SIMPLE INSCRIPTION on a marble tablet in the outside wall of the present Church on Penha Hill does little more than name certain turning points in the history of the Church buildings which have successively occupied that site.

The first Church to be built on this site was the direct outcome of the trade rivalry between the Dutch and the Portuguese when it was rapidly approaching its 1622 climax. For some years previous to that, the Dutch had posted a strong blockading force in the South China Seas between Macao on the one hand and Formosa and the Philippine Islands on the other, with the object of harassing Macao's trade routes to Japan.

Left: The belfry outside the chapel in Guia Fort.

Below: A photograph of one of the two notices in bronze letters affixed to the bell. The upper is on the south-west face and the lower on the face next to the chapel wall. Above the latter notice is a miniature image of Our Lady of Guia. Translation of the notices reads as follows:

ESTE SINO FOI FEITO PARA USO DE ESTA ERMIDA DE N.S. DA GUIA EM O ANNO DE 1707 SENDO PREZIDENTE DELLA E CAPITAO GERAL CIDADE DIOGO DO PINHO TEIXEIRA.

NO ANNO DE 1824 SENDO ADMINISTRADOR DESTA CAPELA DE N.S. DA GUIA O COMENDADOR DOMINGOS PIO MARQUES MANDOU POR SUA ORDEM REFUNDIR DE NOVO ESTE SINO QUE SE ACHAVA RACHADO POR MUITAS PARTES ACRESCENTADO MAIS METAL DE COBRE AFORMEZEANDO ASSIM NA FIGURA COMO NA VOZ. FOI IGUALMENTE SAGRADO E BAPTIZADO COM OS NOMES DE MARIA PELO EXMO BISPO GOVERNADO DFR. FRANCISCO DE N.S. DA LUZ CHASSIM AOS 30 DE JUNHO DA ERA UT SUPRA.

This bell was made in 1707 for the use of the Chapel of Our Lady of Guia, Diogo do Pinho Teixeira being President [Governor] and Captain-General of the city.

In the year 1824, Commander Domingos Pio Marques, being the administrator of this Chapel of Our Lady of Guia, ordered this bell, being cracked in many places, to be recast, thus improving both its appearance and its sound. It was also consecrated and christened with the names of Mary by the Most Excellent Bishop and Governor, Dom Friar Francisco de Nossa Senhora da Luz Chassim, on 30 June of the above year.

CONSTRUCTED
IN
1934–1935
IN REPLACEMENT
OF THE ORIGINAL CHAPEL
BUILT IN 1622
AND REBUILT IN 1837

An English translation of the inscription.

A *photograph of the Penha Church inscription.*

In July 1620, three Portuguese ships laden with silk and other China produce sailed from Macao for Japan. When off Formosa they were sighted by four ships of the Dutch blockade. Two of the Portuguese ships had sufficient speed to avoid an engagement, but the third, the *S. Barthollemeu*, (under Captain Jorge da Silva), did not have this advantage of speed. Faced with these seemingly overwhelming odds of four to one, Captain da Silva and seventeen of his men, who all

had financial interests in the venture, sought help from heaven. They made a vow to Our Lady of Penha de France that if they returned to Macao in safety, they would pay to the Convent of St. Augustine there a sum of money equal to 1% of the value of their cargo, provided that with this money the Convent would build a hermitage in Macao to Our Lady of Penha. Confident in their religious beliefs they prepared for action.

The Dutch planned to capture the ship and

seize her cargo, rather than to destroy her, and to this end they ranged their gunfire on her masts and sails, and not on her hull. But this enabled da Silva to outmanoeuvre them and when the Dutch guns could not be brought to bear on him, he was able to make good his escape. On their safe return from Japan to Macao in 1621, Captain da Silva and his friends redeemed their vows by offering to Friar Estevao da Vera Cruz (Prior of the Augustine Convent then occupying the site next to that on which the Church of St. Augustine now stands) the promised money. Prior Vera Cruz obtained from the Senate a grant of land on the top of Penha Hill, where there had previously been a small fort; there he built the Chapel of Our Lady of Penha (The Rock). The Hermitage was opened and blessed on 29 April 1622 by Prior Vera Cruz who also celebrated the first mass there. It had this in common with the Guia Chapel that they were both built on the summit of high hills, and because of their difficult approaches, they were both favoured by seafarers wishing to redeem vows made during danger at sea, and many of these enhanced their devotion by making the pilgrimage to the hilltops and back, barefooted.

All the three buildings mentioned in the commemorative tablet as having occupied the Penha site have provided living accommodation for clergy in addition to that required by the Chapel. The original one, it will be remembered, was a hermitage. Up until Dom João Paulino de Azervedo e Castro was appointed in 1903, the Bishop had always resided in the Largo de Sé alongside the Cathedral. But during his administration of the See, Dom João moved his residence to Penha, and it has been the Bishop's residence ever since. He was succeeded in 1920 by Dom José de Costa Nunes and it was under his instructions and guidance that the 1934–1935 reconstruction was carried out. He was an art-loving divine, and it may well be that the palace was well designed for internal use, but it can hardly be claimed to satisfy one of the major demands of an architect that his design should meet the demands of the environment as well as those of its principal function. Professor Boxer refers to it as 'a modern Manueline monstrosity in the Portuguese architectural equivalent of stockbroker's Tudor'. Dom José thus certainly left his mark on the physical as well as the ecclesiastical architecture of the Church in Macao. He left there in 1941 to become the Patriarch of Goa, a post which he held from 1941 to 1953. He was appointed Cardinal in 1961, the first Macao bishop, in the long period of 400 years, to reach that eminence.

Located just below the church at Penha, on the lower terrace on the northern side, is an old granite cross, inscribed with the date 18-5-1900. It is now very overgrown and surrounded by banked leaves and weeds. The church of Penha itself is rather neglected, and its principal use these days seems to be a vantage point for the numerous tour buses that come to take advantage of the view which Penha affords. The building itself is in need of repairs. Indeed in its present condition, it looks much more precarious than the structure of the lower terrace and the surrounding garden walls, both obvious legacies of the nineteenth-century building which the present structure succeeds. With age and neglect, the shoddiness of the church's structure, implied in Professor Boxer's acidulous description from decades ago, is increasingly apt.

BARRA

THE BARRA WAS the first fort to be built by the

Portuguese in Macao, and its construction was probably begun about 1613. *Barra*, in Portuguese, means the entrance or the bar of a harbour. In Macao, it was the name given to the headland which guarded the entrance to the Inner Harbour; the name was therefore applied also to the fortress and its chapel which were built on the headland. It lies immediately to the east of the rocky outcrop which had become the site, many centuries earlier, of the Chinese temple of Ma-Kok-Miu from which Macao ultimately derived its name. Until then, the defences of the young colony consisted of a series of strong points protected only by earthworks. When the fort walls were built, they spread far up the southern slopes of the Barra hillside, but the Chinese, fearful lest such strong fortifications might, at some future date, be used to their own disadvantage, forced the Portuguese to cease building before the full plan was completed. It was still unfinished when the Dutch attacked Macao in 1622, and some of their ships shelled its defences — and those of S. Francisco and Bomparto as well — in their feint attack to divert aberration from the real landing at Cacilhas Bay. After this invasion was driven off, the Chinese withdrew their objections to the erection of a fort on the promontory, and the Portuguese ultimately completed their fortifications there in 1629.

When the small chapel was built in the fort, it was dedicated to St. James, the patron saint of Portuguese arms, and a life-size plaster cast of him, helmeted and armed with sword and shield, is still to be seen in a niche in the chapel wall. It was in this fort that Captain-Major Lopo Sarmento de Carvalho held his meagre forces until the intention of the enemy in the battle of 1622 became clear, and it was from here that he reinforced, at the most opportune moment, those mostly irregulars,

engaging the enemy near Guia. It was this counter-attack, led and inspired by Lopo Sarmento himself giving Portugal's famous battle-cry: 'St. James and at them', which was the *coup de grace* of Macao's victory that day. This fortress also had the distinction of having been associated, however indirectly and however long after the event, with another important Macao victory; it was commanded by Colonel Mesquita twenty-five years after he had, as a gunner subaltern, saved the colony from Chinese attack at Passaleão on 25 August 1849.

It is doubly fitting for a statue of St. James to adorn the chapel of this Portuguese fort in Macao, for in addition to being the patron of Portuguese arms and the patron saint of Spain, St. James was believed to have been responsible for bringing Christianity to that country and through it, to the rest of western Europe also. The Portuguese thus associated St. James with their early colonization of Macao in the double hope that he would continue to bless their ventures in arms and at the same time ensure that they were just as successful in bringing Christianity to eastern Asia as he was in introducing it to western Europe.

That St. James is still the patron saint to whom the Portuguese look for help during times when martial strength is needed was made plain at the end of the civil disturbances in Macao in 1966; then many members of the civil population visited this little Chapel of S. Tiago in Barra Fort to return thanks to its saint for the delivery of their city from the dangers of civil strife.

The old Fortress of São Tiago da Barra was converted into the Pousada de São Tiago in the late 1970s, and has retained most of the character and features of the old fort. The chapel with its old image of the saint was incorporated into the design,

The statue of St. James (S. Tiago), depicting him draped and armed as a centurian, standing in a niche in the small chapel in Barra Fort.

and is still to be found there, looking out over Lappa and the entrance to the Inner Harbour.

BOMPARTO

THE FORT OF BOMPARTO was built on another headland at the western end of the Outer Harbour, and was one of the first forts to be built in Macao in replacement of an earlier strong post. The Dutch knew of its existence too when they attacked the settlement in 1622, and it is also mentioned in a letter written on 23 March 1623 in which the new Hermitage on Penha Hill is described as 'overlooking the bastion of Bomparto and its Chapel of Our Lady of Bomparto'.

The stones which tell the story of this fort are depicted below. In the right foreground are the natural granite rocks which form part of the seaward end of the headland mentioned above. Immediately behind these are portions of the old fortress walls and to the left is the modern retaining wall built to allow the Rua da Praia do Bomparto to be continued past the headland along the Outer Harbour shore to link up with the road which used to run from the Inner Harbour only as far as Barra. This foreshore road-link between Barra and Bomparto was completed in 1911, the year following the founding of the Republic, and was appropriately named Avenida Republica. The opening of this road is commemorated by a roadside stone that can be seen both *in situ* and in detail in the photograph below, standing at the foot of the curve of the retaining wall. On it are cut the letters 'O.P.' (*Obras Publicas* — Public Works Department), and the date '1911'.

Left: It shows a modern retaining wall built on part of the site of the former Fort of Bomparto where Rua da Praia do Bom Parto becomes Avenida da República. *Right:* The inscription on the roadside stone.

In the heyday of the foreign East India Companies in Macao, the view of the Outer Harbour very frequently recorded on canvas by artists was one painted from a point near the Bomparto headland, often including its rocks in the foreground. It depicted the western end of the Praia Grande and its graceful sweep along the half-moon shoreline to the S. Francisco headland in the east. The picture by George Smirnoff (see plates) depicts one of these early nineteenth-century views, and a photograph recently taken from approximately the same view point, but a century and a half later. A comparison of these views shows how narrow the Praia Grande originally was, and from other sources it is known that also were its side branches which led off from its western end near Bomparto, into the high ground between the Outer and Inner Harbours. They were narrow steep roads, like the *Calçada* (Cobble-stoned) *Bom Jesus* still is, which led to the col just north of Penha Hill, from where other roads dropped steeply down to the Inner Harbour. En route the branches from the Praia

Grande provided access to the large residential area stretching along the hillside from the East India Company's factory (十六柱, *Shap Lok Chu* or Sixteen Pillars) near S. Lourenço Church, past Bomparto where the Bela Vista Hotel now stands, to Dent & Co's house, now the official residence of Macao's Governor. The other land link between the two harbours was from the middle of the Praia, along what later became the comparatively level Avenida de Almeida Ribeiro from the Praia Grande, past the Leal Senado to the on the Inner Harbour. From the eastern end of the Praia Grande the Rua do Campo led north through the gate in the city wall to the Campo, or open fields, the large flat, bamboo-covered area to the north-east of the city between Guia hill and The Monte which figures so frequently in Macao's early history.

SÃO FRANCISCO

THE OLD FORTRESS of São Francisco, now completely inland, was built to defend the northern end of the Praia Grande and Outer Harbour area at the same time at the fortress of Bomparto was constructed to guard its southern approach. The buildings above the ramparts formerly housed the Franciscan Convent. It is known in Cantonese as Ka Si Laan Pau Toi (加思欄炮台).

Following the extinction of the religious orders in Portugal in the 1820s and their subsequent expulsion from their residences, the old Convent of St. Francis was appropriated by the military and remained in use in that capacity until the withdrawal of Portuguese troops from Macao following the '1-

2–3' disturbances in December 1966. The former Officer's Mess, the attractive Clube Militar, was built in 1871 and has recently been restored.

The old field-pieces on the embrasures on the ramparts of São Francisco have not overlooked the waterfront since long before the Second World War. Now largely hidden away behind the new buildings of the Hotel and Casino Lisboa, and dwarfed by a flyover, it it difficult now to remember that this fortress was once built to command the northern approach to the Praia Grande.

Bands from the resident Portuguese garrison stationed in Macao played regularly in the adjacent Jardim da São Francisco until 1935.

MONG HÁ

THIS FORTRESS WAS BUILT at the instigation of Governor Ferreira do Amaral. The stone above the lintel dates its construction from 1851. Construction of a redoubt on the hill of Mong Há was announced in October 1849, two months after the assassination of Governor J.M. Ferreira do Amaral. Construction of the fortress was opposed by the Mandarin at Heung Shan, on the grounds that Mong Há, being outside the walled area of the city was in Chinese territory. The Portuguese response was that the fortification was necessary to guard the barrier gate, which the ridge of Mong Há directly overlooked. By 1852, the redoubt was already in a poor condition, and had to be totally rebuilt between 1864 and 1866. Further additions were made to Mong Há in 1925, when additions were made to accomodate new armaments.

87

Stone recording the date of construction of the Fortress of Mong Há, 1866.

View of the fortress of Mong Há.

DONA MARIA II

THIS FORTRESS also dates from the period of increased fortification in Macao that followed the assasination of Amaral. Chinese motives concerning Macao had been feared for some time amidst the general collapse of goodwill following the Opium War. The cession of the island of Hong Kong to Great Britain following that conflict, and the subsequent opening of other ports to trade with China rendered Macao's old purpose increasingly redundant. The decline of its usefulness to the other powers meant that they were unlikely to intervene should Macao be threatened by Chinese aggression. This perceived lack of external assistance, should it prove necessary, taken together with the death of Amaral, made additional fortification of Macao's northern areas of pressing concern.

Dona Maria II is the smallest of Macao's fortresses, smaller indeed than that at Mong Há, with which is was contemporaneously built. It was built to command the heights above the Bay of Caçilhas, and northwards over the Areia Preta. The fortress is named for the daughter of Dom Pedro I of Brazil and Portugal, born in Rio de Janeiro in 1819. He became King of Portugal on the death of John VI on 10 March 1826, but he refused to leave Brazil and so he had to renounce the throne of Portugal. This he did in favour of his infant daughter, Maria da Gloria, with his brother, Dom Miguel, as Regent. Dom Miguel usurped the throne in 1828 and Maria fled to England. Pedro, however, abdicated the throne of Brazil in 1831 in order to return to Europe to reinstate his daughter, and in this, with the help of Britain, France and Spain, he was successful. Maria was restored to the throne in September 1833 and reigned as Dona Maria II until her death in 1853.

The fortress of Dona Maria II was built under the direction of António de Azevedo e Cunha, and was finally completed in February 1852. It was bombed by United States Air Force planes on 16 January 1943, flying out of bases in South China. It was badly damaged at that time, and never subsequently reconstructed. Macao was formally neutral in the war with Japan, and housed thousands of refugees from both China and the nearby Colony of Hong Kong, which had been occupied by the Japanese since Christmas Day 1941. The integrity of both Macao's territory and neutrality was treated with scant respect by both the Japanese and the Allied Forces when the occasion suited them.

The old fortress was not rebuilt after the war; instead, it was allowed to become overgrown and has gently decayed over the last fifty years. It remains so to this day — a picturesque though rather inaccessable ruin, located just outside the grounds of the CTT compound on the hill above Estrada Dona Maria II. When it was built its guns commanded the beach at Cacilhas, where in 1622 the Dutch made their landing in an abortive attempt to wrest control of Macao from the Portuguese. Now it overlooks the reservoir and the new maritime terminal. It remains so overgrown that only those who know it is there would recognize the existence of any fortification at all.

Foundation stone above the entrance to the Fortress of Dona Maria II, recording the date of construction which commenced in 1851

IN THIS URN ARE THE BONES OF DONA MARIA DE MOURA E VASCONCELLOS AND HER DAUGHTER DONA IGNEZ, AND THOSE OF THE RIGHT ARM OF HER HUSBAND ANTONIO DE ALBUQUERQUE COELHO WHO DEPOSITED THEM HERE COMING AS GOVERNOR AND CAPTAIN GENERAL OF THE ISLANDS OF SOLOR AND TIMOR IN THE YEAR 1725.

An English translation of the inscription.

The running hand inscription on the granite stone mentioned above, which measures 2 feet 6 inches wide by 1 foot 10 inches high.

ANTÓNIO DE ALBUQUERQUE DE COELHO

THE TABLET on page 90 tells a story which involved the eastern Praia region in the first decades of the 1700s. Built into the south wall of the chancel of the Church of St. Augustine, is a grey, coarse-grained granite stone on which is carved the legend shown on the opposite page.

Behind this stone lies an historic urn, whose history discloses an early eighteenth-century story concerning the *fidalgos* who built Portugal's overseas empire, and displays an historic picture of the times and places in which they lived, loved, fought and died. The full story tells much of the organization and administration of both the Church and the State of their day, both from the secular and from the ecclesiastical point of view, and it makes this stone one of the most enlightening and interesting single stones in Macao's historic collection.

Antonio de Albuquerque Coelho was born of a noble father, but the lineage of his mother, who 'had a son for her cradle ere she had a husband for her bed', was as speculative and obscure as his father's was certain and socially acceptable. The acknowledged father, at the time his son was born, was the Captain-Major of Para and Lord of the Manor of Santa Cruz do Camuta in Brazil; but what his mother's blood lacked in hereditary evidence of noble origin, it made up for in the variety of its national contributors; these sprang from Pernambuco negroes, American Indians and white Europeans in proportions which would be of no consequence now, even if they were known to Angela de Bairros, for such was her simple name. But all these facts were of little moment and of small significance to the Portuguese nobility of the times — about 1682.

The boy was given his primary education by the parish priest of his birthplace, Santa Cruz do Camuta, following which he was sent to Portugal to finish his education. Then, as was expected of younger sons of noblemen or of most sons of his status, he went to India to seek his fortune. He sailed from Lisbon in March 1700 as a marine, which was the usual practice with *fidalgos* on their first tour of service in the Orient, on a voyage that was to last for six months, and was to be a fatal one for a record percentage of the souls on board. It was an ominous introduction for him to life at sea in the Orient at the turn of that century. Promotion came to him after his arrival at Goa, again routine, and in 1706, when he sailed for Macao, he did so as a Captain of Marines in the frigate *Nossa Senhora das Neves* (Our Lady of the Snows).

The ship was under the command of Captain Jeromino de Mello Pereira and there were two other *fidalgos* on board besides Albuquerque: Dom Henrique de Noronha and Francisco Xavier Doutel. Dom Henrique was the first lieutenant of the ship and was described on his arrival in Macao as a *cavalheiro* (gentleman). Doutel was a well established Macao merchant, having first come out to Macao from Portugal in 1698. He was born in Braganza and one of his direct ancestors earned patriotic fame for his defence of the Castle of Braganza against the Spanish when Philip II of Spain took over Portugal in 1580.

Doutel's personal history is a small window through which we may catch an undistorted glimpse of Portuguese life in Macao in the early eighteenth century. On the business side he had, in less than ten years, become a wealthy trader and shipowner, despite heavy shipping losses which included the *Santa Cruz*, burned at Cavite in the Philippines Islands, with the loss of many of the crew, and another which was taken by Arabs as far west as the Arabian Sea, in the Gulf of Cambay off Surat.

The Portuguese community in Macao formed only a small percentage of its total population, and the number of those who were of gentle birth was even much smaller still, and as it was not possible to bring out from Portugal sufficient prospective wives to meet the needs of all the bachelors, the families of the gentry of Macao inevitably became highly interrelated. Doutel's marriage to Francisca Pereira was an example of this interrelation and made him a close relative of the wealthy de Moura family. As a consequence of this shortage of young ladies from Portugal and the presence of a number of noble families with a surplus of ladies of all ages, sizes and adaptabilities (many of them with reputedly large dowries), Macao earned for itself the reputation in Portugal's empire in the Orient of being a happy hunting ground for impecunious bachelor *fidalgos* in search of rich partners.

Such was the Macao of 1706 when it was the destination of these four members of Portugal's gentry. It is not known how well these four were acquainted with one another when they sailed as shipmates from Goa, but by the time they arrived at Macao they were irrevocably divided into two pairs of friends, each pair being enemies to the death, of the other. Unfortunately, the voyage ended by their ship encountering a typhoon just south of Macao and in consequence she entered Macao on tow on 26 August, a mere hulk, mastless, rudderless, riggingless and 'without even a beakhead'. But what was more unfortunate still was that the damage sustained by the frigate was so great that the repairs took two years to complete and that during this long enforced stay in Macao, the enmity between Dom Henrique and Albuquerque developed into a feud which might well have cost the latter his life.

In Macao, Albuquerque went to live in the mission house of the San Franciscan friars on the headland at the eastern end of the Praia Grande. Dom Henrique, on the other hand, lived with the affluent Doutel, and this brought him into friendly relationship with the de Moura family with whom Doutel was connected by marriage. It so happened about this time that the most sought-after of the unattached Portuguese girls then was Maria de Moura e Vasconcelos, and her dowry was so large that the fact that she was only nine years of age made no difference to the ardour of her suitors whose number was increased by two with the arrival of the frigate *Nossa Senhora das Neves*. Both Albuquerque and Dom Henrique became ardent suitors for her heart and eager aspirants for her money. Such Macao love-matches were treated as very serious games by Macao's Portuguese community, and any one of noble birth in the colony could take as active a part in the game as he or she wished and on whichever side he or she chose. Consequently from the 'line up', one could gauge fairly accurately the status and chances of the contestants. Albuquerque, for instance, had on his side Bishop Casal and most of his clergy, as well as the Jesuits, and the captain of the ship. Dom Henrique, on the other hand, could muster the Dominicans, the Papal Legate (the Patriarch of Antioch who was being detained by force temporarily in Macao), a host of past suitors who were naturally antagonistic to anyone who looked like winning where they had failed, and the girl's grandmother, Maria de Vasconcelos. She was a strong ally for any suitor to have because her granddaughter, being an orphan and a minor, was her ward and thus her partiality to Dom Henrique was an understandable consequence of her family connection with Doutel. This family relationship is set out diagrammatically in the following chart.

With Dom Henrique having the advantage of the family support, Albuquerque had ultimately either to resort to the use of force or to retire from the contest altogether. Having the Church and his own armed men on his side, he chose the former line of action. In June 1709, he forced his way in the grandmother's house, seized the willing Maria and took her to the parish church of S. Lourenco where they were betrothed by the Vicar General,

Lourenço Gomes. Dom Henrique took his time and carefully planned his response. But unfortunately for him, it was not so skilfully executed. A few weeks after the betrothal, Albuquerque was one day returning on horseback along the Formosa to the Franciscan Convent when he was shot at by a negro slave employed by Dom Henrique; but the slave's aim was bad and the unscathed Albuquerque turned his horse and bravely tried to run his assailant down, but the slave made good his escape up a side street. Albuquerque resumed his journey towards S. Francisco, and again he was shot at, but this time his assailant was Dom Henrique himself, using as

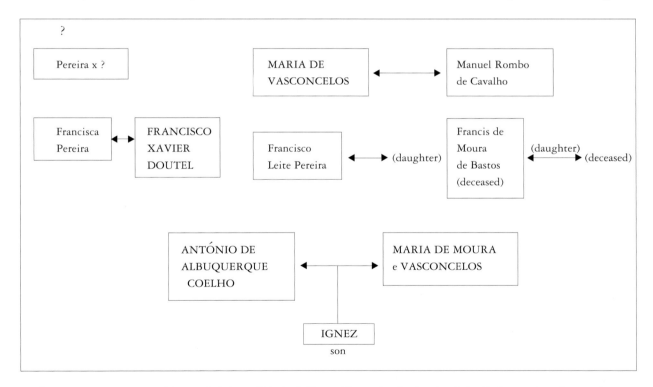

A diagrammatic representation of the genealogical tree of Maria de Moura e Vasconcelos, showing the relationship between the main actors (names in capital letters) in the de Moura drama.

cover a house at the eastern end of Rua Formosa, situated where the Catholic Centre now stands. Dom Henrique's aim was better than the slave's and Albuquerque was wounded in the right arm just above the elbow. He was able to ride on to the Convent however, but on the way he was attacked a third time by another of Dom Henrique's slaves whose aim was just as wild as the first one. Albuquerque managed unaided to reach the Convent but there he had to be helped from his horse and immediately treated by the ship's and the Senate's surgeons, who unfortunately made light of the injury. But Albuquerque's good fortune did not desert him; ten days or so later an English East-Indiaman arrived at Macao, and the surgeon on board, on being asked to see him, immediately warned Albuquerque's friends that gangrene had developed in the wound and advised that if the patient's life was to be saved, the arm should be amputated without delay.

But before agreeing to undergo this operation, Albuquerque wrote to Maria asking whether she would still marry him, even without his right arm; to this she 'made the classic reply that she would marry him even if his two legs were cut off, so long as he was still alive'. This episode naturally stilled a lot of mischievous tongues but it nevertheless spurred his opponents on to greater efforts, while a local poet was moved to write the following stanza which survived as a Macao folk-song for many years; here it is given both in Portuguese and in English:

Nao he tao formosa,
Nem tao bem parecida,
Que, por seu dinheiro Maria arma tanta briga.
She is not so beautiful,
Nor yet so fair,

That for her money Maria should cause such a stir.

Maria's grandmother, who would have probably been antagonistic to the marriage of her granddaughter at such an early age whoever the suitor, decided to join the battle in the open. So during Christmas 1709 she attempted to end Maria's engagement to Albuquerque by requesting the Senate to assume legal responsibility for her granddaughter on the grounds that Albuquerque intended to abduct her in his frigate to Goa. This move was a source of no small embarrassment to the Senate because the relations between the four official parties in Macao — the Senate, the armed services, the Church and the Governor — were very delicately poised, and the Senate could not afford to act openly against the Commander of the frigate who was known to be actively supporting his officer by supplying the loving couple with protective guards. The Bishop snubbed the Senate for their suggestions and the Governor reacted by surrounding the Dominican Convent with soldiers when Dom Henrique fled there to be immune from arrest. Eventually, on 22 August 1710, the nine-year-old Maria became the bride of Albuquerque in the Casa de Campo de S. Francisco. This 'house' was used as shore barracks for officers and men of naval craft when in Macao and its amenities naturally included a chapel. The wedding took place in this chapel and was quietly solemnized by the Chaplain of Albuquerque's frigate. These special arrangements undoubtedly foiled a last desperate attempt to assassinate the bridegroom, for it was discovered later that an ambush had been set for him outside the Church of St. Anthony where Dom Henrique had reason to believe the wedding would take place.

In 1712, a daughter, Ignez, was born to the

twelve-year-old Maria, but the baby survived only one week. Two years later, the birth of a son was the signal for magnificent celebrations which were repeated on 27 July 1714, the day of the infant's christening. But these celebrations were cut short four days later by the death of Maria from puerperal fever. In spite of the sympathy this bereavement won for Albuquerque from among his fellow citizens in Macao, and in spite of their respect for the way in which he began to use his newly-acquired wealth for the benefit of the poor and needy, his enemies persisted in persecuting him and succeeded in having him arrested. He was imprisoned in Guia Fort by Manuel Vicente Rosa, then Ouvidor of Macao, but he was later released and went to Goa to face the charge of 'tyrannous behaviour not only to the citizens of Macao but equally to the foreign nationals who sought to trade in that port'. Of this charge he was totally exonerated and instead of his career being ruined, he was appointed to be the next Governor and Captain-General of Macao. This was a turn in events not very much to the liking of Doutel, who, as misfortune would have it, was the owner and captain of the ship in which the new Governor was to return to Macao to take up his post. Apparently, Doutel could not face the ordeal of making another voyage with Albuquerque, certainly not under the new circumstances, so on the night before the ship was due to leave Goa, Doutel, without notifying his distinguished passenger, suddenly gave orders for the ship to sail on the pretext of having to avoid a threatening storm. Albuquerque made an amazing overland crossing to Madras in order to catch another ship from there, only to encounter such difficulties in Malaya that he did not arrive at Macao until 30 May 1718, exactly twelve months after leaving Goa. He assumed office the next day and when

Doutel, who had also been delayed en route and had been forced to winter in the Indies, arrived back in Macao, he found Albuquerque had already been installed as Governor. Whereupon Doutel, fearing the worst, took refuge in the Franciscan Convent, but Albuquerque magnanimously made no attempt to use his new position to redress either past or recent wrongs committed under such different circumstances. Other adversaries spread the story that Albuquerque had secured his appointment by bribery and would use it for his own selfish ends, but they were completely mistaken. His governorship was later described as the best and most popular held 'under the reign of the Braganzas'; but this savours rather of oriental hyperbole, for as it took the first twelve months of his appointment to reach Macao, he spent only a little over one year in actual service in the post before his successor arrived, and he would need to have been an extremely talented man to justify such a reputation in such a short time. His early service gave no evidence of this outstanding ability but it did prove him to be a determined and courageous officer, and this probably accounts for the fact that on his return to Goa, he was immediately given what was then an extremely difficult assignment, the Governorship of Timor and Solor. This appointment he held with undoubted distinction from 1721 to 1725, and on relinquishing this post he took the opportunity of revisiting Macao, arriving there on 29 September 1725 and staying with his friends, the Franciscans. On 23 November, they celebrated a mass for his wife and daughter, and at the end of the service, the bells of all Macao's churches were tolled, and minute guns were fired from the Monte Fort, in memory of his young wife Maria and Ignez, their daughter. It was then that he deposited their bones, together with those of his own right arm — amputated in 1709 — in an urn which he then committed to the safe-keeping of the Convent Church of S. Francisco. There it remained until 1865 when this Church was demolished to make way for the barracks which now occupy that site; it was then transferred to the Church of St. Augustine where for over a century now this commemorative stone has impartially kept the memory green of the girl-wife and of her *fidalgo* husband, of their enemies and of their friends alike, and will continue to tell their story while the Church and its stones remain.

A reference to Albuquerque, written in January 1746 in a biographical sketch of the principal *fidalgo* at Goa, reads:

> Antonio de Albuquerque Coelho, son of Antonio de Albuquerque who governed Angola and the Mines, aged over sixty years, a widower without issue [sic]. He has occupied various posts with distinction and courage, and governed Timor, Macao and Pate with the rank of General and with prudence and skill. He was finally General of Bardes, which post he resigned to live amongst the Franciscan Friars of the Province of the Mother of God, where he is now leading a devout and holy life. He is very clever, honest and truthful.

FRANCISCO XAVIER DOUTEL

FRANCISCO XAVIER DOUTEL spent all 47 years in the Orient in the service of his country, and like Bishop Casal, it was in the Orient that he died. He undoubtedly had ability and courage above the average and with it he accumulated experience and a wealth of this world's good things, also well above the average. From these mental and material stores, he could afford to contribute much to the needs of his less fortunate fellow compatriots, and this he did liberally. In the afternoon of his life he also gave freely to the church, especially as the feud, in which he and Bishop Casal had taken opposing sides, was now long since a thing of the past. He built a chapel in Macao which, because of the particularly large Stations of the Cross that it contained, he named *Bom Jesus* (The Good Jesus). It was built on the top of the col just to the north of Penha Hill and gives the name to two small neighbouring streets, *Calçada Bom Jesus* and *Travessa de Bom Jesus*, as well as to the *Mount of Bom Jesus* and to the *Carmel*, later to occupy the site. In addition to his religious philanthropies in Macao, Doutel's service to the Portuguese communities in the Orient of nearly half a century, included public office in both Macao and Timor. In the former he was Ouvidor for a term, and in the latter he served as Governor. He eventually died in Timor in 1745 or 1746.

After his death and those of his relatives who survived him in Macao, the chapel was left uncared for and fell into ruins. The site remained untenanted for many generations and historic references to it ceased and their places were taken by imaginative stories of pirates, hidden treasure, ghosts and spells. Early this century, it was bought by the Chinese Maritime Customs, as a site for a new residence required for the Commissioner in Macao, but it was never used for that purpose. While it remained the property of the Maritime Customs it was used as a wild garden, or as a romantic playground by children. Later in the bishopric (1920–1941) of Dom José de Costa Nunes, he hoped to build a hospital on the site, but at that time there was no one of Doutel's financial stature who could contribute the amount of money required for such a project, so the site remained unoccupied until 1941 when it was acquired by the *Carmelitas*

Descalças (Barefooted Carmelites) who still occupy it. It can be readily appreciated how this wild entanglement of trees, shrubs and tall grasses, standing isolated behind a high wall for over a century, could easily become haunted by many variations of its own true history.

The children of the Chinese Maritime Customs Commissioner at Macao, Colonel Francis Hayley-Bell, spent a large portion of their childhood during the early 1920s in this garden. The elder of them, Mary Hayley-Bell, mentions in her autobiography the stories current among her parents and their friends as well as the Chinese servants, regarding the history of *Bom Jesus*. These stories all show the typical signs of variations due to the frequent retelling, over long periods, of tales whose origins have long since been shrouded in mystery. Certainly the story of Doutel's life lends itself to such treatment — his wealth gained from trading with places spread wide over the Orient, whose names alone were enough to stimulate fancy; his frequent visits to Arabian waters and his ultimate departure for the South Seas never to return; his Macao chapel uncared for and unused until tropical vegetation closed in on it and hid all evidence of the details of its former grandeur. Could this be the origin of the story that 'on this very hill, behind its wall, now a tangle of trees, faded grasses and cactus bushes, there had once existed, centuries ago, a temple dedicated to the sea and sea rovers'. This sounds more like either Ma-Kok-Miu or Penha, but the rider which added that the last of the Sea Gods with his final breath 'laid a curse on any man who should so much as break the soil in this Holy ground' makes it difficult to associate it with either of these or with *Bom Jesus*, all of which show today no sign of such a curse. But the flight of narrow stone steps 'leading from nowhere to nowhere half

buried in the accumulation of age old moss and leaf mould', found by the Hayley Bell children in the early 1920s, may well have belonged to Doutel's chapel.

Here we must stop following the historic trails to which Maria's memorial directed our feet, and in spite of the engaging stories of bishop's palaces and fields of operation of important people through which these trails have led, the central figure of the drama was, and must remain, the sad short-lived girl-mother, whose emotions had not matured enough to enable her to differentiate between the love for a husband and her worship of a hero adventurer.

FAÇADE OF ST. PAUL'S COLLEGIATE CHURCH

OF ALL MACAO'S STONES, none is more eloquent, none speaks with a voice more forlorn, yet has a message of more hope, than those which speak from the ruins of this church façade. These stones are all that remain of Macao's greatest work of art — an architectural gem of the early seventeenth century. Tourists and travel agents alike have made the picture of this façade, rising majestically and defiantly towards a sky of tropical blue, the universally accepted pictorial symbol of Macao. Perhaps but few travellers returning from South East Asia realize that in their postcard and photograph albums and slide cabinets at homes, they must certainly possess at least one pictorial record of the relations between Macao and Japan as expressed by this architectural symbol; it is an historic reminder of the part, disastrous as well as beneficial, played by the rival churches of Spain and Portugal in the Orient.

We have already seen how and why the success of the early Portuguese trade with Japan was in the main responsible for Macao's initial prosperity and development, and that this trade arose out of the peculiar triangular situation that existed between the Chinese, Japanese and the Portuguese. For the subsequent change in this flourishing trade and its effect on the prosperous city of Macao, the stones of the St. Paul's façade and of the memorials set up at various times within the church confines have much to say.

The first Christian missionaries to land in Japan were three Jesuit priests and a Japanese convert, under the leadership of Father Francis Xavier, SJ, 'The Apostle of the East'. The party was given passage from Malacca to Japan in 1549 in a ship whose owner-captain was a Portuguese merchant named Jorge Álvares. The ship put in at Kagoshima in Kyushu where the Jesuit passengers were given a welcome no less enthusiastic than that extended to the traders themselves. However, after twenty-seven months of missionary endeavour, Francis Xavier returned to Malacca disappointed with his achievements in Japan and disheartened with the prospects there. But shortly after his return, he heard again the missionary call, this time of China's millions, and in 1552 he gave heed to it and re-embarked with the same Jorge Álvares in his ship the *Santa Cruz* for China. Álvares took his passenger only as far as the island of Sheung Chuen where he left him to await a permit to enter China proper. But this aim Francis Xavier never achieved, for he died on the island before his permit arrived and his remains were taken back to Malacca the next year by the same Captain Álvares in the same ship, *Santa Cruz*.

This Jorge Álvares must not be confused with his namesake of a previous generation, the first Portuguese exploring navigator to reach Lintin in the Canton delta. Yet, it was to such a misunderstanding as this that we owe the presence in Macao today of the statue of the elder Jorge Álvares. As a result of the researches being conducted a few years ago into the early history of the explorer, the premature announcement was made that his birthplace had been located in a small village near the Spanish border in the Province of *Trás-os-Montes* (Behind the Mountains), called *Freixo de Espada a Cinta* (a Tree with a Sword-belt at its Waist). The joy of the village elders knew no bounds when they heard this news, and they decided to erect a monument in their town to the memory of its most illustrious son. Money was readily forthcoming for the project and when the fund was oversubscribed, the village elders decided to offer a replica of the original to the Colony of Macao. The offer was gratefully accepted but by the time the statue arrived in Macao, further researches by Father Teixeira, who had a personal interest in the project as he was also a native of the same town, had revealed the fact that it was Captain Jorge Álvares of the *Santa Cruz* who had been born in *Freixo de Espada a Cinta,* and not the explorer. As far as we know none of the three famous men — Jorge Álvares the explorer, his namesake the merchant-captain or Francis Xavier, SJ, — had ever set foot in Macao, yet indirectly they all had much to do with one or other aspect of Macao's early development. The statue of Álvares the explorer is the most fitting single statue to represent the services to Macao of this trio and it was because of a simple historical mistake that we are prompted, when we look upon this statue, to recall the work of three men, Álvares the explorer, Álvares the merchant-captain and Francis Xavier, the Jesuit missionary.

Had Francis Xavier been too impatient about

the time the Christian seed was taking to germinate in Japan? If so, subsequent events proved he had sown better than he realized. When he decided to return to Malacca, his three original companions remained in Japan and largely as a result of his sowing and of their labours, by the end of the century, there were estimated to be approximately 300 000 Christian converts in Japan. But numbers do not tell the whole story. The Japanese claimed that some of the priests who subsequently joined their earlier colleagues were intolerant and bigoted, and that their influence over their converts made these latter place the loyalty they owed to their country second to that accorded to their newly-adopted religion. Eventually, by 1587, under the Shogunate of Hideyoshi, Jesuits were considered to be a threat to the security of the state and they were all banished from the country while the Japanese people were forbidden to accept the Christian faith. But, because this drastic action would have meant the loss to the Japanese of much of their valuable Portuguese trade as well, the Shogun refrained from demanding strict enforcement of his orders. Instead, he adopted the amazing procedure of introducing European opposition by allowing three Spanish priests, who arrived from the Philippines in the disguise of envoys, to enter Japan.

This was in 1593, and although Spain and Portugal were then united under one Crown, the national animosities and the religious jealousies that existed in Europe between the Portuguese Jesuits on the one hand and the Spanish Franciscans and Dominicans on the other, broke out afresh in Japan. The Portuguese particularly resented the presence of the Spanish in Japan because they claimed it contravened the Pope's gift of the sole right of proselytizing in Japan to the Portuguese Jesuits; it also broke Portugal's trade monopoly.

Japan, for a decade or more after the arrival of the Spaniards, was seething with disturbances that arose between the two resulting groups of Christians converts and also with those due to the Japanese persecution of Christians in general. The period 1626–1633 were years of particular terror for all Christians in Japan: in 1624 the Spanish were expelled; in 1636 Japanese were forbidden, under pain of death, either to leave (or if they had done so inadvertently), or to return to their country; in 1637 Christianity was entirely proscribed and in 1639 any Portuguese merchants and priests still in the island empire were finally expelled.

It is ironic to think that it was the rivalry between these Christian groups, as much as the threat of Christian beliefs to the national allegiance of their converts, that made Japan decide to go into complete seclusion from the rest of the world for a period which was to last for two centuries, especially as this was just at the time when the maritime nations of the West were carving overseas empires out of the Orient with their territorial expansions; but it was not:

> . . . the purely religious aspect of Christianity, that finally brought about the proscription of the Christian religion with all its tragic and far-reaching consequences. In the eyes of the Japanese rulers it was a subversive force, much as Communism is regarded in the countries of the free world today; and ruthless though the measures taken to suppress it were, they were no more so than those adopted by the Spanish Inquisition or by the Portuguese and others of that period. Religious tolerance was unknown in any land during the sixteenth century.

This illustrates the ethical problem raised by the freedom of action often exercised by zealous missionaries and justified by them on the grounds of their various religious beliefs. In addition to these examples in Japan, we shall have occasion later to mention more cases of trouble caused by missionaries acting at variance with laws or treaties in order to proselytize their own particular form of Christianity in China. Western merchants were quick to criticize the missionaries for this, but their own actions in attempting to impose their Western trading methods on the Orient were open to exactly the same criticism.

We have already noted that the people of Macao during their heyday of Japanese trade did not relax their search for other markets in the Orient; this far-sighted policy meant that when the lucrative trade with Japan came to an end, Macao had already established alternative markets. She then became almost solely an *entrepôt* for intra-Oriental trade, excepting in so far as she allowed other European powers to use her port facilities for their intercontinental trade. By this means the various European East India Companies were able to gain and maintain a footing in Macao. The Pacific trade that Macao set up was with Manila, and through it, to Mexico and Peru, with Indo-China, Java and Siam, and with fringe islands in the East Indies like the Celebes and Timor. It was this trade that tided Macao over from the silver era of her Japan days to the more mundane era when it was to the advantage of the other European merchant traders to keep her on the Orient stage.

The façade of St. Paul's is an important landmark in the history of Macao's churches and of her church architecture, but it also marks an important stage in the history of her trade with Japan and of that country's closure of her doors against all foreign missionaries and traders. With the church in the forefront of all Portugal's advances of discovery and of commerce in the Orient, priests found their way up to the China coast in the vicinity of Macao soon after Albuquerque arrived in Malacca in 1511. It is recorded that there were two priests working near the mouth of the Pearl River as early as 1521, and from then on there was a constant stream of priest working in the South China coastal areas. It would appear that the first priest to settle for any length of time in Macao was a Spanish cleric, Father Gregorio Gonzalez, who worked there continuously for twelve years, arriving about 1557 or soon after.

The first Jesuits who came to Macao to make it their permanent field of labour were a party of three, consisting of Father Francisco Perez (Spanish), Manuel Teixeira and Brother Andre Pinto, both Portuguese. They arrived in Macao on 29 July 1563 and in December of that year established their temporary residence in a house owned by Pero Quintero. By the end of 1565, they had acquired the site which is at present occupied by the presbytery of St. Anthony's Church, and on this site, next to the hermitage of St. Anthony, they built a residence and a church. These buildings were of the 'matshed' type of structure, commonly used throughout South East Asia — roof and walls of palm leaves supported by a frame of bamboo or pine — but these were destroyed by fire and their replacements were built of wood with tiled roofs.

In 1579, the Jesuits were given another site on a low hill near The Monte and on its slopes they erected another residence which was later to become a Jesuit College. Then in 1582, they built a new church on the top of the same low hill where the present ruins stand, and the church and the college were dedicated to the training of priest for the conversion of the Japanese. Another Jesuit house was built alongside the earlier residence in 1580 with funds donated to pay for the training of Chinese priests for missionary work in China. On 1 December 1594, it was decided to divide this Jesuit community into two, each section under its own administration, the church and the college of St. Paul comprising one section devoted to the training of missionaries for Japan, the other to the training of missionaries for China.

In 1601, fire again caused further grave material loss to the Jesuits in Macao, but this time only the church was completely destroyed although the adjacent college and residential buildings were seriously damaged. One compensation was the way in which the merchants and the public of Macao alike rallied to the aid of the priests in their effort to make good the loss. The story is vividly told in the Annual Report for the year 1601–1602, a portion of which reads:

. . . besides the alms given by many persons (notwithstanding the fact that it was a time when the city was in extreme necessity, many men having lost almost all their wealth in a ship which disappeared during the return voyage from Japan), all the inhabitants of the city, being moved by charity and compassion, called a meeting before the Captain-Major, in which they decided by universal consent to contribute to the house of the Jesuits one half per cent of their possessions in Japan providing our Lord return the missing ship, for which everyone was waiting, from Japan safely. It was then learned that the missing ship which they were expecting had returned. This was very good, because God returned the ship with a very profitable cargo, and the charity amounted to no small sum, the total being three thousand one hundred and thirty *pardaus de reales.*

VIRGINI MAGNÆ MATRI
CIVITAS MACAENSIS LIBENS
POSVIT·AN·1602·

TO THE GREAT VIRGIN MOTHER, THE MACAO COMMUNITY, OF ITS OWN FREE WILL, SET UP [THIS STONE], AD 1602.

The Latin inscription on the foundation stone of St. Paul's Collegiate Church. An English translation of the inscription is shown on the right.

The outside view of the south-west corner of the ruins of the church, showing the façade (extreme right) and wall (centre and left) and the stone. The illustration shows the difference in structure between the façade and the wall. The former is of granite while the adjoining portion of the latter is of grey Chinese brick, the rest of the wall being made of red earth, sand and lime. These ingredients were mixed with water, placed in the wall mould, tamped down hard and then allowed to set. This gave the finished surface the stratified appearance seen in the photograph.

The rear view of the façade of the St. Paul's Collegiate Church, showing the remains of the church walls, and above, the line of the roof of the former church. This asymmetrical line shows that the façade was not designed for the church it eventually adorned.

The rebuilding of the church was begun, and the commemorative stone laid in 1602. Advantage was taken of the presence in Macao at the time of a number of skilled artists and artisans among the Christian refugees from Japan, and the plans for the church and façade were the work of an Italian Jesuit, Father Carol Spinola. The financial depression due to the stoppage of Japanese trade interfered, however, with the building plans and the Jesuits had to be content with a much less elaborate church design than that of Father Spinola. The church was completed towards the end of 1603 and it was opened, midst great rejoicing and gratitude, on Christmas Eve of that year. It was not until 1620 that enough money — 30 000 silver taels — became available for the building of the façade. Work was thus begun on it twenty years after the church itself was finished, resulting in the different structures in the stone façade and the brick and mud walls, shown on page 102. The façade was not completed until 1640 so that Father Spinola never saw the creation of his mind other than on paper, for he was martyred in Japan in 1623.

The church was beautifully decorated within with wood carving and paintings, also the work of refugee artists from Japan, and for over two centuries it reigned unchallenged as the most famous occidental building in the East; and then it, too, fell to the greatest enemy of wooden structures — fire. On the evening of 26 January 1835 at 6 p.m., fire broke out in the kitchen quarters of the college and by a quarter past eight nothing remained of the college and its church but the façade and portions of the church walls. The walls unfortunately were considered to be a public danger and eventually much of them had to be demolished, and thus only

the façade was left to bear witness to Macao's part in Portugal's attempt to introduce Christianity, Western culture, and trade to Japan; it stands therefore as a memorial to the thousands of Japanese and European Christians who perished in persecutions rather than deny their faith, and as a reminder that Macao is a religious, as well as a martime haven of refuge.

But the stones of the Jesuit Collegiate Church of St. Paul have more to tell than the changes in its history due to the fluctuations in its physical fortunes.

In 1759, troubles between the state and the Jesuit Order came to a head in Portugal, and in the end, decrees were issued dissolving the Society in Portugal and her colonies. These decrees were not put into effect in Macao until 5 July 1762 when, on that day, all the possessions of the Order, both property and money, were confiscated by the Crown, and all its members still there were arrested by the army. The Church of St. Paul was placed in charge of a rector appointed by the Bishop and the college buildings were taken over by the Senate. For a time from 1798 onwards, a regiment of the army was quartered there and it was in the wood supply in their kitchens that the disastrous fire started on 26 January 1835.

The church thereafter consisted only of ruined walls and the façade, so on 8 April following the fire, the Senate decided to use it as a temporary place of interment for bodies awaiting final burial in their own parishes. The administration of these new uses to which church floor and its walls were put was handed over on 14 May 1836 to the *Santa Casa da Misericordia*. This charitable institution, which held its quatro-centenary celebrations in October 1969, supervised the building of catacombs

103

in the thick, ruined walls, and the preparation of the rest of the former church area for use as a cemetery for the poorer and pauper members of the Catholic community.

The first burial in this church cemetery under the new organization was on 30 May 1837, and on 1 June its administration was taken over by the Bishop and remained in use as a cemetery until 2 November 1854. After that date, many of the identifiable remains, together with their memorials, were transferred to the new public cemetery of St. Michael, but some of the memorials were left *in situ* at St. Paul's, and as this was no longer consecrated ground, other memorials (for example, some of those from Penha Hill Armenian burial site) were moved there; thus the enclosure of the former Church of St. Paul became to all intents and purposes, an outdoor historical museum. With the administration of the property back in the hands of the Senate, that body had to spend a considerable sum of money on rendering the area safe for the public who were making increasing use of the precincts as an open space. The ruined walls constituted a danger, especially as these were further weakened by the excavations made in them for burial niches. The walls were first reduced to a height of twenty-five feet and later removed altogether, excepting those parts behind the façade which were left as buttresses, and as such still stand today. The façade was thus rendered reasonably safe from Macao's main building hazard — the typhoon — but unfortunately it provided no protection for the memorial stones from pillage or from vandalism. Sad to relate, many of these memorial stones disappeared, some to reappear in local buildings or road construction work, while others were sold by unscrupulous citizens to shipowners for use as ballast

and were later recognized from their inscription when they were being laid as pavement stones in Manila. After the receipt of these reports, more care was taken of the remaining memorials and they were kept safely in the St. Paul's site until after the 1966 riots. These disturbances made it plain that even here these stones were far too accessible to modern vandals. A special interest was subsequently taken in the preservation of these memorials and arrangements were made for their removal to a safer location. Unfortunately, the workmen engaged in moving them did not appreciate that preservation was the underlying motive for their removal. Some of the memorials were large and heavy granite slabs — one was over eight feet long — and these the workmen proceeded to break into smaller pieces in order to facilitate their removal.

Stone fragments, lying in the Flora Gardens, photographed as an example of stones that may well have a story to tell. It was subsequently found they had indeed a valuable story to tell, for they were stones that had been rescued from the precincts of the former St. Paul's Collegiate Church after the December 1966 riots. Their stories cover the years from 1578 to 1853.

Fortunately, a watchful employee of the Leal Senado was able to rescue a number of these pieces and the photograph on page 104 depicts one heap of these rescued stones lying in the Flora Gardens awaiting their chance to retell their story. When these fragments were sorted out and pieced together, it was found they formed major portions of eight engraved stones and one Dutch statue. Five of these stones, whose dates range from 1578 to 1835, were Portuguese, and these we now describe in chronological order.

GEORGE BOTELHO – died 1578 AD

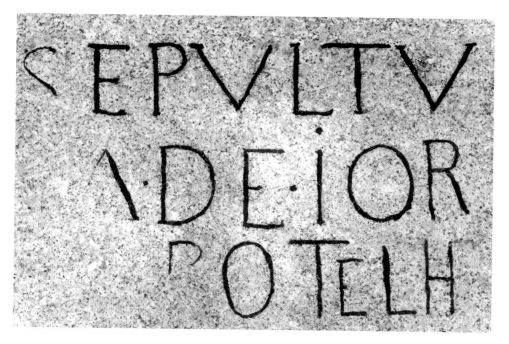

SEPULTU [R]
A.DE.IOR [GE]
BOTELH [1578]

TOMB OF GEORGE
BOTELHO [1578]

*A photograph of the oldest personal memorial so far discovered in Macao. The lettering on the stone is now incomplete; the full inscription in Portuguese, with the missing letters enclosed in square brackets, is given on the **right (upper)**. The date, no trace of which can now be seen on the stone, was fortunately obtainable from other sources.*

The stone is a thick (7 inches), almost square (2 feet 5 inches wide and 1 foot 11 inches high), slab of grey, coarse-grained granite, and is known to have at one time being in the Church of St. Augustine. However, this could not have been the original burial site as this church was not built until 1587. It is not known when the stone was moved to St. Paul's, nor is any personal information concerning George Botelho available. This stone has obviously been a paving stone and was placed in such a position that only its left hand bottom corner has been exposed to a constant stream of traffic. This exposure has been long enough to erase all the lettering to the left of a line passing diagonally across the inscription. It has erased the lower part of the letter S in the top line; the letter R and the left limb of the letter A in the second line; the letters GE, the dot and the lower part of the letter B in the third line; and the letter O at the end of the name BOTELHO must have been at the beginning of a fourth line. If the date ever was cut on the stone, it was at the beginning of the fourth line, following the terminal letter O of BOTELHO, as the stone is not long enough for the date to be centrally placed and yet be included in the erased zone. If it was cut at the beginning of the fourth line as 578, a date form used in that period (see page 105), it and the missing letter O would easily fall within the erased zone.

ANGELA DE LUS – died 1621 AD

To date no information is as yet available concerning Angela de Lus and her husband Simon Conrado, nor is anything known for certain concerning the significance of the devices depicted on the uppermost fragment of this memorial. Authorities in Portugal consulted do not think they represent

grenades nor can any reference to a military organization which would have used such a device, be found in Macao records. In any case, the reduplication of the device makes it more likely that they represent the two divisions of the family referred to in the inscription, husband and wife and male and female relatives. The dividing line separating the two figures would favour this explanation rather than the military one, but even so its significance remains unclear and uncertain. The figures of the date, 621, in the last line of the inscription are symmetrically placed and the omission of the thousands digit is therefore obviously intentional. It was a date contraction in fairly common usage among the Portuguese at that time, similar to our custom in these days of writing '68 for 1968.

SEBASTIAN ÁLVARES – died 1645 AD

Above the inscription (but not shown in the photograph) just under the top edge of the stone, is carved in low relief the pontifical coat of arms — crossed keys surmounted by the Papal crown. This indicates that Father Álvares had some official connection with the higher administrative bodies of the church.

Towards the end of 1641, Álvares became involved in a difference of opinion between the Governor of the Bishopric of Macao, — then Friar Bento de Cristo, OFM, and Pe Gaspar Luiz, SJ, Commissioner of the Holy Office. On the orders of the former, given in December 1641, the sub-deacon — Paulo Teixeira, a native of Salcete, a small town near Goa — was excommunicated and imprisoned in the tower of S. Lourenço Church. Shortly afterwards, Teixeira escaped from his confinement and successfully sought refuge with

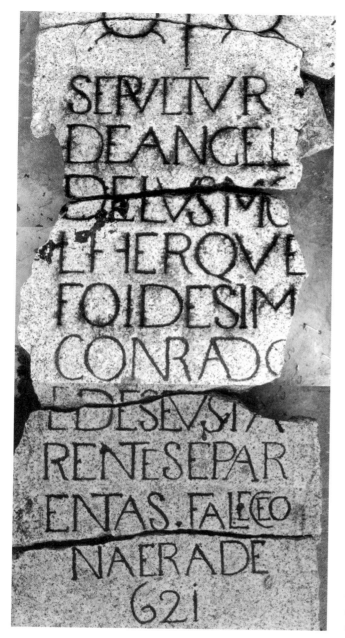

SEPVLTVR[A] DE ANGEL[A] DELVS MO LHER
QUE FOI DE SIM[AO] CONRADO E DE SEUS [PA]
RENTES E PAR ENTAS FALECEO NA ERA DE 621

TOMB OF ANGELA DE LUS WIFE OF SIMON
CONRADO AND OF HER MALE AND FEMALE
RELATIVES DIED IN THE ERA 621

Left: Five of the fragments of the memorial of ANGELA DE
LUS. It is 7 feet long, 2 feet 6 inches wide and 4 inches thick,
and cut out of grey, coarse-grained granite. **Right:** The inscription
is reproduced in Portuguese with the letters missing from the stone
indicated by square brackets. Translation of the inscription in
English is given below the Portuguese. Since this photograph was
taken, a further stone fragment has been found which carries the
rest of the final O in line 6, proving the name to be CONRADO.

107

the Jesuits in St. Paul's. The Governor of the Bishopric demanded that the escapee should be handed over to him, but this the Jesuits refused to do. In January 1642, Father Gaspar Luiz became Principal of the Jesuit College and he adhered to the previous decision of the members of his Order not to surrender their refugee, in spite of the arguments and entreaties of the Governor of the Bishopric. Finally the latter sent two envoys, Fathers Sebastian Álvares and Manuel Pereira armed with two lengthy memorials written to convince the Jesuits of the justice of this action. Father Gaspar

Luiz accepted the letters but not only ignored their contents, but won over the two envoys to the Jesuit point of view. Then, towards the end of January 1642, they, along with twelve other priests, met to elect a new Governor of the Bishopric. This highly unconstitutional action was doomed to failure, and Friar Bento de Cristo, acting promptly, publicly excommunicated all the participating priests, including Father Álvares.

Little further is known of the personal history of Father Sebastian Álvares excepting that time healed the trouble between him and authority, and that on his death in 1645, this memorial stone was first set up in a cemetery near the Church of St. Lazarus belonging to the Cathedral. From the wording of the inscription describing him as it does as 'an outstanding benefactor of this Church', it would seem that he was fully reinstated before his death.

A QUI IAS O R.P.SE BASTIAO ÁLVARES CLERICO PRESBI TERO THEOLOG PREGADOR CURA QUE FOY DA SE IN SIGNE BEMFEITOR DESTA IGREIA QUE FALECEU AOS 8 DE JULHO NO ANNO DE 1645

HERE LIES THE REV. PADRE SEBASTIAN ÁLVARES CLERIC PRESBYTER THEOLOGIAN PREACHER, PRIEST OF THE SEE OUTSTANDING BENEFACTOR OF THIS CHURCH WHO DIED ON 8 JULY IN THE YEAR 1645

*Left: Three fragments of the memorial stone of Father Álvares, showing as much of the inscription as can now be deciphered. **Right:** The full Portuguese wording and a free translation of it in English. The granite is grey and coarse-grained, and the stones are rough-hewn at the sides and the back, and average 6 inches in thickness, and 2 feet 7 inches in width. The overall height of these pieces when placed together is 4 feet.*

DOMINGOS MARQUES – died 1787 AD

Domingos Marques was the son of Manuel Francisco Marques and was Procurador of Macao from 1783–1784. His wife was Maria Francisca dos Anjos Ribeiro Guimaraes, the daughter of João Ribeiro Guimaraes and Inacia de Oliverira Paiva. He was Procurador at the time when the Armenians were given permission by the Augustinian hermitage at Penha to have their own burial ground — the first to be given to foreigners — on Penha Hill, and it was his son, Domingos Pio Marques, who represented Macao at the coronation of King John VI at Rio de Janeiro in 1818.

SEPULTURA DE
DOMINGOS M[ARQUES
DE SUA] MULHER MARIA
RIBEIRO GUIMARAES
FILHOS E HERDEIROS O
QUAL FALECEO NO
ANNO DE 1787

TOMB OF DOMINGOS
MARQUES, OF HIS WIFE
MARIA RIBEIRO
GUIMARAES,
DESCENDENTS AND
HEIRS, WHO DIED IN
THE YEAR 1787

Left: A photograph of the inscription on three pieces of the memorial of DOMINGOS MARQUES, which was approximately 4 feet high and 2 feet 7 inches wide. It is of grey, coarse-gained granite and has been left rough-hewn at the back with an average thickness of 6 inches. The damage involving the second line and the date is of very recent origin, the edges of the upper and lower pieces of stone having been chipped off when being moved for identification and matching, but fortunately the letters and figures have already been deciphered. Right: The reconstructed Portuguese inscription, and its English translation.

ASSOCIAÇÃO PIEDOZA DE S. FRANCISCO XAVIER

The 'Pious Association' was the Fraternity of St. Francis Xavier, founded in 1812 to celebrate the Feast of St. Francis Xavier and to help the poor of Macao in his name.

Its members and supporters were mainly Macao merchants and after some initial years of successful work, it was decided to apply for official recognition of the fraternity and approval of its regulations. Accordingly in 1819 Constantino Jose Lopes, Pedro Candido dos Santos Vital, Bras Joaquim Botelho and Canon Antonio de Macedo sent copies of the regulations to Senhor Arriaga Brum de Silveira, then Ouvidor of Macao, together with a request that they be forwarded to the competent authority for recognition. The papers were eventually passed to Rio de Janeiro where King John VI was residing during Napoleon's occupation of Portugal. Royal assent was given in 1833 and when this was received in Macao, arrangements were made to inaugurate the now official fraternity. The celebrations to mark the inauguration were held in 1835 and the stone was placed in the Church of S. Lourenco to commemorate the occasion. It must have been moved to St. Paul's during one of the periods of renovation of S. Lourenco. Nevertheless, the church is still the centre of the fraternity, and the Feast of St. Francis Xavier is still celebrated there each year and its funds still provide for the poor of its parish.

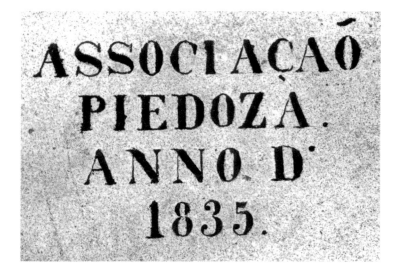

PIOUS
ASSOCIATION OF ST. FRANCIS XAVIER
AD 1835

Left: *A photograph of a stone slab, measuring 2 feet 2½ inches wide, 1 foot 6½ inches high and 7½ inches thick, of light grey, fine-grained granite. The surface of the stone has been polished and the letters are beautifully cut in deep, vertical-sided, broad-based incisions.* ***Right:*** *An English translation of the Portuguese inscription.*

110

THE VICTORY MONUMENT

ON THE WESTERN SIDE of Guia hill, in a small park extending between Avenida de Sidónio Pais and Estrada da Vitória is a monument to the victory that safeguarded Macao at one of its most critical periods, and thus guaranteed that Macao would not go the way of so many other Portuguese possessions in the Far East, from Malacca to the Moluccas.

Macao for the first forty years of its existence was completely unfortified. No defences were necessary as the Portuguese with their superior weaponry were more than a match for any local pirates. The *wako*, the Japanese sea-marauders who had so terrified the Chinese coast in recent centuries, had been largely extinguished. In any case, the Portuguese were the carriers in a extremely profitable trade been Japan and China, with Chinese raw silk being exchanged for Japanese silver bullion. The Portuguese traders, being at this time on excellent terms with the Shoganate, had little to fear from any vessels originating from Asian waters.

There were, however, other nations in Europe whose merchants were becoming aware of both the immense profits to be made from trade in Far Eastern commodities, and of the precarious and mostly undefended position of the Portuguese trading *entrepôts* with whom they dealt. The English saw the advantage of seizing Portuguese stations and taking all the profit for themselves; so too did the Dutch. In 1598, the Dutch established themselves in a small trading station at Banten on the island of Java, and gradually laid the framework for what was ultimately to become the Netherlands East Indies. From their base there, they harassed Portuguese shipping, passing through the Straits on the journey between Malacca and Macao.

In 1601, the Dutch arrived in Macao for the first time. Word had spread to Macao concerning Dutch attacks on Portuguese shipping in the Straits, and the landing party were captured and a number were later executed. In subsequent years more Dutch ships arrived in Macao, on each occasion to be driven off again to sea.

The Macanese astutely realized that sooner or later the Hollanders would arrive again with a strength of numbers likely to critically outnumber the Portuguese, who in any case had no defensive positions to defend in case of attack. In 1606, work on the seaward defences of Macao commenced and continued apace for some years. The fortifications at Barra, at the entrance to the Inner Harbour, and at either end of the Praia Grande, Bomparto to the south and São Francisco to the north, were set in place. The Dutch had meanwhile established themselves more securely on Java, and had also obtained a trading position at Hirado, not far from the Portuguese station at Nagasaki. They regularly called at Formosa for supplies on their voyages from Java to Japan, and were thus in a position to menace Portuguese shipping travelling between Nagasaki and Macao.

Profit in the Japan trade depended largely on the availability of raw Chinese silk. The most priced came from the silk-producing districts of Shun Tak (順德) in the West River region inland from Macao. Macao traders held the monopoly on this extremely valuable commodity, and the Japanese were insatiable in their demand for it. From their bases on Formosa, raw silk was only obtainable sporadically and at a very high price from Chinese pirates. The Dutch, therefore, resolved to capture the silk market at its source and planned an invasion of Macao.

In June 1622, a Dutch invasion fleet appeared, intent on capturing the city from the Portuguese.

On the 23rd, they attempted to effect an entry into the Outer Harbour by bombarding the forts defending it. In this they were unsuccessful, and after a battle lasting the entire day, they withdrew after the loss of one of their ships.

The next day, 24 June, was the Feast of St. John the Baptist. In the morning, they renewed their bombardment of the shore defences, though this time it was intended as a feint. At the same time as attention was diverted to the Outer Harbour, their main force landed at Cacilhas Bay, at the northeastern end of the peninsula, beyond Guia Hill and out of sight of the main fortifications. From there, meeting only slight resistance, they advanced towards the undefended edge of the city.

When the defending Macanese realized the situation, all available strength was brought to bear upon the Dutch who were advancing along the muddy path through the fields. The Jesuit Fathers in their fortress-seminary on The Monte brought their guns to bear on the advancing Dutch force. As they advanced towards the lower slopes of The Monte, one of the Jesuits, Father Rho, by a feat of extraordinarily good marksmanship scored a direct hit on the Dutch powder magazine, which blew up with a tremendous explosion, killing and maiming all around it.

The Dutch continued to press their attack, but being short of ammunition they halted at the main entry point into the city, between the hills of Monte and Guia, and prepared to take one of them in order to secure a position on higher ground. When the Portuguese realized that the Dutch did not intend to attack the Praia Grande, they sent reinforcements to that side. With the nation's battlecry 'São Tiago', the Portuguese charged down on all sides upon the hapless Dutch invading party, who were completely routed. The Dutch commanding officer was amongst the first to be killed, and after his death the others were swiftly routed. Many of the Dutch were killed, others were taken prisoner, and still more drowned trying to reach their boats. The victory was complete. The next day the Dutch sent a party under flag of truce to ransom their prisoners, but this being refused they sailed away.

The large flat area lying between the Guia and The Monte, where the Jardim da Vitória is situated, was the battleground where the Dutch and the Portuguese fought. It is still known to the Chinese population of Macao as Ho Laan Yuen (荷蘭園), or the field of the Dutch. Long commemorated only in local legend, a monument in stone was finally erected to the victory over the Dutch, almost two hundred and forty years after it had taken place.

GARDENS, FOUNTAINS AND WELLS

MACAO UNTIL RECENT YEARS has had no purely decorative public fountains, nor has it any fountains which trade for coins under the guise of tourist wishing-wells. What fountains have as a reference to the past are natural springs and wells, rather than decorative fountains; waters that give rather than receive, that originally served the domestic needs for water of the nearby poor households, rather than the camera needs of well-to-do sightseers.

Two of these springs and one well figure in the early Portuguese history of Macao, and yet a third spring is prominent in the history of the work of the first Protestant missionary in China two centuries later. The first two springs and the well are mentioned in the account of the Dutch attack

PARA PERPETUAR NA MEMORIA
DOS VINDOUROS
A VITORIA
QUE OS PORTUGUESES DE MACAO
POR INTERCESÃO DO
BEMAVENTURADO
S. JOÃO BAPTISTA
A QUEM TOMARAM POR PADROEIRO
ALCANÇARAM
SOBRE OITOCENTOS HOLANDESES
ARMADOS
QUE DE TREZE NAUS DE
GUERRA CAPITANEADAS
PELO ALMIRANTE ROGGERS
DESEMBARCARAM NA PRAIA
DE CACILHAS
PARA TOMAREM ESTA CIDADE
DO SANTO NOME DE DEUS DE
MACAO
EM 24 DE JUNHO DE 1622
NO MESMO LOCAL ONDE
UMA PEQUENA CRUZ DE
PEDRA COMEMORAVA
A ACÇÃO GLORIOSA DO
PORTUGUESES MANDOU
O LEAL SENADO
LEVANTAR ESTE MONUMENTO
NO ANO DE 1864

The Victory monument in the Jardim da Vitória.

(In spite of the date on the stone, the monument
was in fact only put in place in 1871.)

Close-up of the inscription on the Victory monument.

113

on Macao on the morning of 24 June 1622 for they supplied the cooling waters which tempted the Dutch soldiers to make these springs the real, as well as the metaphorical, turning point of their advance inland.

The association of a garden with history is likewise self-evident when it is founded in memory of a specific historical figure or event. But when the garden actually takes part in such an event, its historic importance may in the course of time be forgotten unless it is memorialized by stone or in print.

FLOWER FOUNTAIN

FLOWER FOUNTAIN, as the *Fontenário da Flora* is known in English, is one of these springs. It is easy of access, being situated a few yards to the east of the north end of the Avenida de Sidonie Pais, close by the entrance to the *Jardim Municipal da Flora* (Flora Gardens). It has always been easy to locate; up until a few years ago, it was readily recognized by the long lines of housewives and amahs using its surroundings as their family laundry, or by the continuous procession of children and coolies replenishing their household supplies of drinking and cooking water.

Nowadays however, the area is no longer used as a laundry, but adequate identification is just as easily achieved and in a much more sanitary manner, by displaying the name of the fountain on the tanks in which water is stored while awaiting distribution to users. This distribution is controlled by two taps, one issuing from the mouth of each of two granite tigers crouching below the name.

These two stone heads are still there to be seen at the entrance to the Jardim Municipal da Flora.

These days the water is no longer used for purposes of washing and bathing, but the fountain itself has a small and unrecognized function as a wishing well. There are always a few coins of low denomination to be seen in the bottom of the tank — witness to the many who visit the attractive and quiet park every day.

ALFREDO AUGUSTO DE ALMEIDA

ALSO CONTAINED within the Flora Gardens is a memorial bust of Alfredo Augusto de Almeida, who rescued from destruction many old stones found lying about in various places in Macao. Alfredo Augusto de Almeida was born in Macao in 1898, the son of a distinguished and long-established Macanese family. An amateur naturalist and botanist of some note, Almeida worked for the Department of Public Works for many years, and it was due to his interest and enthusiasm for plants and gardens that Macao's public spaces are as lovely and well-planned as they appear today. He was responsible for the reconstruction of the attractive gardens at the Church of St. Lawrence, work which was completed in 1935. He was also responsible for the preservation of many old stones, whose varied and interesting stories are detailed elsewhere in this volume, that were destined for destruction, and rescued from oblivion by his atention to the history of Macao.

In the dark days following the 1–2–3 December turmoil in Macao, many visible reminders of the Portuguese presence were removed. In some cases, as with the pedestal of Mesquita's statue in the Largo do Senado, with the wish to forestall further agitation for which they could be seen as an excuse or provocation. Others were removed, ostensibly

The Fontenário da Flora at the entrance to the Flora Gardens.

for their own safekeeping. The fact that preservation was the object of the exercise was not mentioned to the workmen involved in their removal, and a number were badly smashed and broken. Almeida, recognized the importance of the preservation of these stones for posterity, and endeavoured to have them preserved for future generations. Their efforts resulted in a number being set into the walls of the Leal Senado, and others being resited in the fortress of Monte.

A
ALFREDO AUGUSTO DE ALMEIDA QUE EM VIDA
TANTO AMOR DEDICOU A ESTE JARDIM
1898–1971.

Alfredo Augusto de Almeida
Whose life was dedicated to the love of gardens
1898–1971.

An English translation of the inscription on the bust of Alfredo de Almeida at the Jardim Municipal da Flora.

FOUNT OF ENVY

THE SECOND OF the two springs was situated at the upper end of a short lane — Rua da Fonte da Inveja — which starts at the Avenida de Sidonie Pais about one hundred yards to the south of the *Fontenário da Flora*, and ends in a cul-de-sac on the lowest slopes of Guia Hill. It was named the *Fonte da Inveja* or the Fount of Envy or Jealousy because all the other springs which issued from the Guia hillside were envious of the purity of its waters. Long before the other springs were harnassed at their outlets, an imposing façade had been built for the Fonte da Inveja, and this must have increased the jealousy of the others especially as its waters were made to issue through the lips of a more-than-life-size copy in granite of a Roman head.

But alas, this envy of all the other Macao springs no longer gushes from the Guia hillside, its waters having either dried up altogether or they have been captured by another underground stream and issue elsewhere, perhaps from the neighbouring spring in the Flora Gardens. Its once imposing façade has regrettably been allowed to fall into disrepair and its base has been silted up to such a height that the date of its last renovation — 1918 — can only with difficulty be uncovered and deciphered.

The site of the former Fonte da Inveja has now been completely obliterated, and is the exit point of the Guia Tunnel. The tunnel was completed in 1980, and now the only reminder of the old Fonte da Inveja is in the name of the approach road to the tunnel on the Avenida Horta e Costa side, Rua da Fonte da Inveja.

To complete our description of the Guia hillside waters which the Dutch soldiers found so satisfying on a mid-summer morning in 1622, we must refer, but briefly, to the well mentioned above. It is in the eastern corner of the Jardim da Vitoria, close to the stone retaining wall along the top of which runs the Estrada da Vitoria. The water still has to be drawn manually, but the muddy surroundings which are so often found near wells of this type have been abolished by protecting the mouth of the well with a 2-foot high stone or brick rim which is covered by a substantial cement surface.

FOUNT OF SOLITUDE

THE THIRD SPRING was the one at which Dr Robert Morrison baptized the first Chinese Protestant convert. He was Tsae Ah-ko, the younger son of a Macao shipowner, and he and his elder brother, Tsae Low-heen, were given a good education by their father until he lost most of his money when his ship disappeared on a trade mission to Batavia. Not long afterwards the father died and the two brothers were thrown on their own resources. Ah-ko was only sixteen years old at the time and his education had suffered somewhat by chronic ill health. However, the elder brother, Low-heen, obtained employment with the Dr Robert Morrison as his tutor and assistant soon after the latter's arrival in Canton on 7 September 1807. It was not long before Morrison met the younger brother Ak-ko and he at once recognized him to be a young man with character and ability above the average. When Morrison's translation of the Gospels and the Acts of the Apostles was ready for printing, Low-heen obtained employment for his younger brother with the blockmaker, Leung Ah-fah. This gave Ah-ko access to the literature which he had so often heard being read and discussed at religious services held in Morrison's house. It was about 1811 that Ah-ko decided that he would like to be

Left: *The neglected remains of the former façade built at the Fonte da Inveja.*

Right: *The Roman head which formerly controlled the water outflow from the façade. Fortunately however, the granite head has been saved and now reposes in more congenial surroundings in the nearby Flora Gardens.*

baptized, but Morrison did not consider that he was yet ready for such a step. Family and business difficulties caused further delays so that it was not until 1814 that Morrison was satisfied that Ah-ko was ready for baptism. Morrison was in Macao at the time and his entry in his diary for 16 July 1814 reads:

> At a spring of water issuing from the foot of a lofty hill by the seaside away from human observation, I baptized, in the Name of the Father, Son, and Holy Spirit, the person whose name and character has been given above.

The hill was Guia Hill and the stream was the one which provided water for a drinking fountain — *Fonte da Solidão* (the Fountain of Solitude).

This fountain did not mark the site of the Tsae Ah-ko's baptism. This took place at the foot of the hill where the steep descent of the stream ended in placid pools before its waters ultimately reached the sea across a wide beach which has since been replaced by a very much wider reclamation. The fountain was built half way up the hillside where the stream crossed the Estrada de Cacilhas, and the photograph reproduced on page 118 shows the leafy site and the fountain as they were in 1908.

117

The Fonte da Solidão as it appeared in 1908.

Fonte da Solidão is now merely a memorial, for it no longer functions as a fountain and has lost much of its former glory as well as its life-giving streams. The innumerable trickles of water which united on their emergence from the hill to form the stream, were mostly diverted when munition tunnels were built into the hill alongside the fountain shortly after World War II. But modern progress has sounded not only the death knell of its use; it has done the same to the appropriateness of its name as well. Solitude is no longer a fitting name for it, but it always will remain a fitting memorial name. Yet, strange as it may seem, the latest and worst offender in the banishment of solitude from Macao — the Grand Prix — has brought the name of this memorial back into almost general use. It is safe to assume that only a very small percentage of Macao's modern generation have ever heard of Fonte da Solidão, and much safer to predict this to be true of all her visitors. But now, the road in front of the old fountain forms part of the racing circuit, and nearby are some S-shaped bends which are of importance to the racing motorist and therefore of interest to the enthusiastic race followers. In order to facilitate the task of race description, a name had to be found for this stretch

118

of the circuit and it was supplied by the unused fountain and its forgotten name. In racing parlance, the nearby portion of the road is known as the *Solidão Esses*. Some of the evidence of its earlier glory, however, has been saved for posterity in the form of a pair of granite lions which, it is claimed, formerly guarded the fountain head. If this be so, the photograph taken in 1908 proves that they must have been removed before that date. Nevertheless, whatever be their early history, these lions now rest from their labours in permanent retirement with the other historic stones in the Flora Gardens.

GRANDMOTHER'S FOUNTAIN

IT REMAINS NOW but to close this brief survey of certain of Macao's fountains by a reference to one that is today only an historic memory. It stood in Largo do Lilau, a cobblestone-covered square in the fashionable foreign quarter of a century and a half ago which sat astride the spur separating the Inner and Outer Harbour residential districts. It is reported to have been one of Chinnery's favourite sketching sites, but whether that was because it was within but a short walking distance of his residence or because it appealed to his artistic taste, is hard to say. A fountain was certainly located here by 1795, and the spot had been the site of a known spring, which provided water for the small hermitage at Penha, first established in 1622. Locally famous, the fountain was known as the Fonte do Lilau (sometimes spelt Nilau) — the Grandmother's Fountain.

The fountain, or rather the spring from which it drew its source, gave rise to a very old and popular Macanese saying concerning both it and the magical powers of attraction to this corner of the world, enough to draw those who drank from it forever back again to Macao.

Quem bebe água do Lilau
Nao mais esquece Macau:
Ou casa cá em Macau,
Ou então volta a Macau.

Who drinks from the water of Lilau
Can never leave Macao:
Their home is in Macao,
They will always return to Macao.

No description remains to us of the fountain of Lilau. Almost certainly its design would have been practical, rather than decorative. It was probably a wall fountain, the type generally favoured in Macao, an example of which is to be seen in the courtyard at the rear of the Leal Senado.

It is doubtful, however, whether the Leal Senado fountain was ever a functioning one. It is more likely to be a copy of one that was in use elsewhere in the city — as for example, perhaps, in Largo Lilau — and was considered so important historically that on its demolition, a replica was erected in the Leal Senado.

The replica to be found in the garden of the Leal Senado consists of two square columns projecting forward for a distance of 2 feet as short wings from either end of the back wall. In the space thus delineated is set the basin of the fountain — roughly rectangular but with its ends and free side, curvilinear. It is 2 feet high, 10 inches wide and extends forward about 2 feet from the wall. The ornamentation is meagre and is of two types. The first is a homogeneous group of roundels carved on the front surface of the basin and of the bases of the lateral columns.

The large replica of a wall fountain standing in the courtyard of the Leal Senado. No evidence is available as to its origin or history.

The other is a heterogeneous group of seven ornaments on the back wall of the fountain. The lowest is a pair of male heads sporting moustaches and markedly wrinkled foreheads, with puffed cheeks as though in the act of blowing water out of the tap in each mouth. Above these is a scroll devoid of any ornamentation or inscription, and above that again, centrally placed, is the Portuguese coat of arms, supported laterally and beneath by two laurel branches. Surmounting this is a crown, while at the sides at a level just above the scroll are two pendent floral designs which appear to be suspended from a substantial support; the pendent design is of three bunches of grapes each hanging behind three single-lobed leaves and between each bunch are carved three small spheres. The significance of these spheres is not clear, but it would appear to be more than decorative for it is repeated below the left hand laurel branch and in the hair fringes over the temples and above the

120

forehead of each of the heads. These heads are the only part of the fountain carved in granite. The rest is cast in concrete.

A new fountain has been erected in the pleasingly restored Largo do Lilau. It is completely flat, and very modern in inspiration, with two fountains of water flowing out to a small pond at its base. The Largo do Lilau is very quiet, and both it and the fountain seem to receive very few visitors.

JARDIM DE SÃO FRANCISCO

THIS GARDEN IS of very ancient origin, and takes its Chinese name Ka Si Laan Fa Yuen (加思欄花園) from the old convent of São Francisco, situated above it. From 1861 until 1935, the gardens were a popular promenade to listen to the military bands which played there. These lovely gardens were a popular meeting point for the people of Macao for generations, and remain so today.

FLORA GARDENS

IN 1857, THIS GARDEN was known to the public as either Father Almeida's Garden or the *Flora Macaense* (Macao Garden), and as such it came under active consideration as a possible site for a new Protestant cemetery. Nothing came of this suggestion however, but another garden — Carneiro's Garden — was bought by the Trustees of the Old East India Company Cemetery instead, and has been used and known ever since as the New Protestant Cemetery. In the meantime, the Flora Macaense property — consisting as it did of a house as well as the garden — was bought by the government of Macao for use as the summer country

The new fountain of modern design in the restored Largo do Lilau.

residence of the Governor, and one of the attractions of the property at the time of its purchase was stated to be that from it, an excellent and uninterrupted view could be had of the Inner Harbour!

Many decades later, the Macao government was able to acquire in its stead, a house and grounds situated in a commanding position above the western end of the Praia Grande, overlooking the Outer Harbour. This was formerly the property of the British firm of Dent & Co., which flourished in Macao during the latter days of the English East

121

India Company and the early decades of Hong Kong; the house became the all-seasons residence of the Governor, and remains so to this day. Father Almeida's former property was thenceforth no longer needed by the government as the governor's residence, and it subsequently passed into the hands of the late Sir Robert Ho Tung of Hong Kong and the gardens are still known among Macao's pedi- and taxi-cab drivers as *Ho Tung Fah Yuen* (Ho Tung Gardens). Today however, while the house has long since ceased to exist, the garden still survives as the Jardim Municipal da Flora. In addition to preserving carefully identified and clearly labelled specimens of most of Macao's trees, shrubs and flowers, the garden has provided safe keeping for many stones which formerly adorned some of her earlier historic structures. Thus this garden has become an important museum for objects, both animate and inanimate, of historic interest to Macao. The same applies also to some of the other Macao gardens, both public and private. Examples of the former are the gardens of Vasco da Gama, of Victory, of Camoens and of Montanha Russa, and of the latter there were those privately owned by Father Carneiro, by João Lecaros and by Daniel Beale, the English trader and long-term resident of late eighteenth-century Macao. The Jardim Municipal da Flora qualifies for inclusion in both categories, it having been at one time privately owned first by Father Almeida and then by Sir Robert Ho Tung, and is now a public garden. The original owner was a parish priest in Macao for many years. Having been born in Portugal, he arrived in Macao and before his death in 1880, many of his leafy memorials were adorning no small number of Macao's streets, parks and gardens. His stone memorial is a plaque on the north chancel wall of the Church of St. Anthony, where he was also buried.

CAMOENS GARDENS

BETWEEN A QUARTER and half a mile directly north of the ruins of the Church of St. Paul, stands a low, well-wooded hill, its base surrounded by the Camoens Gardens. To reach it from St. Paul's, one follows approximately the same line that was taken by an early city wall which ran from The Monte, passing north of this hill, to end at the Inner Harbour. Of this wall the mandarins were extremely suspicious, for they considered it an unnecessary display of strength — possibly aggressive — in an area so close to the isthmus and the border. Under pressure from the Chinese, this part of the wall had ultimately to be demolished by the Portuguese, but the line it followed can still be traced among old-fashioned cobblestone streets in the vicinity of St. Anthony's Church and the Praça Luis de Camoens.

If there can be a counterpart of the Tower of Babel among city squares, this Praça has strong claims for such a distinction, for through the last four centuries its stones have echoed and re-echoed in Latin, Portuguese, French, Spanish, English, German, Dutch, Armenian and Chinese. Before 1558, the natural stones of the Praça had never echoed with any but Chinese voices; but when its first church — that of St. Anthony — was built, they began to echo with Latin and Portuguese as well. These echoes were soon reinforced by voices from the new Jesuit mission which became a neighbour of the Church of St. Anthony in December 1565. Two centuries or more later, their chorus was swelled by the voices from the Canossian Institute, while the memorials in the Casa Garden, the East India Company cemetery and the Camoens Grotto (*Gruta de Camões*) added their own voices in English and various other European languages. The grotto is close to the summit of the nearby hill and is reached by well-shaded and well-graded paths leading from the Camoens and Casa Gardens. On the summit of the hill is a collection of large, granite boulders, many of which are carved with messages in either Chinese, Portuguese, French, Latin or English. The grotto itself is formed by an unimpressive cleft between two clusters of these boulders, and it shelters a bronze bust of Camões — the giant of Portuguese literature. It is an appropriate site for this memorial for tradition has it that some of the poet's epic, *Os Lusíadas* (The Lusiads — The Sons of Portugal) was written there. Even in these days, the disturbing noises from the large modern city below hardly penetrate its calm seclusion, and so in Camoens' days in Macao, it may well have been a place for detached meditation so necessary to poets in their creative hours; but it must also have been an uncomfortably cold and drafty place to live in during the winter, and an impossible one to occupy during the summer wind and rains of the typhoon season. It is hard to imagine the grotto as anything more than a temporary place for seclusion and meditation in daylight hours, and then only during the more congenial months of Macao's inequable climate. But before we attempt to differentiate the truth from the embellishments — or in some cases from complete fabrication and fantasy — of the stories of the grotto and, to a lesser extent, of the memorial, we had better look first at the generally accepted story of the life of Camoens.

LUÍS DE CAMÕES (CAMOENS)

IT IS GENERALLY believed that Camoens was born about 1524, of a family of the minor nobility in Lisbon. However, the date of his death is certain, being agreed by historians to have been 1580. He died penniless and friendless in Lisbon, and was buried there in an unidentified pauper's grave. Yet within twenty years, he was already recognized as Portugal's greatest poet, and within a century or so many of his sonnets and his epic poem had been translated into several European languages, and literary scholars all over the world had come to look upon him as being among the world's greatest epic poets.

He was sent to the Coimbra University for his higher education but at that age his turbulent and impetuous nature had already begun to develop and he had to return to Lisbon without finishing his course. There he fell violently in love with a lady at the court with the result that in 1546 he was banished. He joined the army as a private soldier and served with distinction in action in North Africa. After the loss of his right eye in the wars there, he returned to Lisbon but again ran into trouble at court and was imprisoned in 1552 for wounding a court official. He was released the next year on condition that he promised to leave the country and serve in India. He had already begun writing his major work which included a reference to Vasco da Gama's famous voyage, but it was not until Camoens found that the route his ship was taking around the Cape of Good Hope, followed closely that of the explorer, did he begin to appreciate the real immensity of Vasco da Gama's achievement.

His experience of the mighty storms that raged around the Cape of Good Hope induced him to remodel his poem, making the explorer's achievement of navigation and discovery the central theme of his epic. His description of these storms also became the favourite theme of artists wishing to symbolize with pen, brush or chisel, either Vasco da Gama or his voyage. Until recently, there were two examples of this in Macao. The first still exists as the marble carving in low relief on Vasco da Gama's monument, but the second exists now only in memory or in photographs. It was a picture in blue and white tiles depicting the struggle between Vasco da Gama and the giant Adamastor who sent his tempests in a vain attempt to prevent the explorer from rounding the Cape. The story is told in *The Lusiads* by Camoens, and it is from this poem that the title of the picture is taken — *NÃO ACABAVA, QUANDO UMA FIGURA*, Canto V, Est. xxxix.

In India, Camoens served with Portuguese military forces, but again his satirical pen led to his downfall and the Viceroy, displeased with his cutting comments about Goa, is supposed to have sent him further east with the fleet that was dispatched in 1556 under Francisco Martins to extend Portuguese trade to South China. One report claims that en route to China he made a diversion to the Molucca, where he remained for about twelve months, thereby greatly enlarging his knowledge and experience of Portugal's achievements in the Orient. Montalto de Jesus does not refer to this deviation at all, but he does state that Camoens was with the Portuguese fleet when it was stationed at Lampacao in 1557, and from that concludes that he must have taken part in the operations against the pirates whose defeat led directly to the founding of Portuguese Macao. Even if this be true, it does not constitute any proof that Camoens ever was in Macao, nor is there any documentary evidence extant to the effect that he was ever sent there as 'Custodian of the Property of the Dead and the Absent' (*Provedor dos defunctos e ausentes*). When Camoens left Goa, neither the place nor the name Macao was known to the Portuguese, and the only possible foundation for this report could be that the appointment was to the fleet and that its jurisdiction extended not only to its members but also to any settlements set up ashore under its commander.

A picture, in blue and white tiles, illustrating Camoens' description of Adamastor obstructing Vasco da Gama's passage round the Cape of Good Hope, and entitled 'It had not finished when a figure appeared'.

The claim that Camoens worked and perhaps lived in the Macao grotto which now bears his name depends almost solely on the slender evidence that some of the phrases such as 'secluded spot' and 'embosomed in the rocky cleft', mentioned in one of his sonnets, refer to the grotto in Macao. A translation of Sonnet CLXXXI reads:

Where shall I find a more secluded spot,
Of all delightful traits so sadly bare,
That need I say no man betakes him there,
When e'en by beast it rests uncared, unsought.
Some frowning woods with awful darkness fraught,

Or sylvan solitude of dismal air,
Without a sprightly brook or meadow fair,
In fine a place adapted to my lot.
For there, embosomed in the rocky cleft,
In life entombed, there freely may I mourn
O'er plaintive, death-like life of all bereft,
Save tears and woes to which there is no bourn.
In cheerful days there shall I feel less sad,
Contented too when all in gloom is clad.

Wherever the truth in all these claims and counter-claims may lie, it is certain that Camoens could not have stayed in Macao long enough to write much of his *Lusiads* there, for he again fell foul of authority and was sent back to Goa in 1559 to face a charge of maladministration, whether while with the fleet or in Macao is not known. If in the latter, the charge might well have been substantiated if it could be proved by his accusers that he spent much of his time in a cave far removed from the centre of the growing settlement and from the problems confronting the 'Custodian'. But plain sailing was not a characteristic of any of his life's journeys, and in this case the disturbing factor was shipwreck near the mouth of the Mekong River. All that Camoens saved out of this disaster was his life and his manuscript, and this he achieved by the amazing feat of accomplishing the long and dangerous swim ashore from the wreck unaided. Because of this setback, his arrival in Goa was delayed until 1560. Here, and in Mozambique, he suffered further delays, with the result that he did not reach Portugal until 1570.

Safe at home at last after an adventurous absence of over ten years, Camoens devoted himself assiduously to the publication of his literary works. They appeared in print in 1572 and were an instant success, his lyrics and sonnets themselves being sufficient to win for him a place among the greatest Portuguese poets. It was his epic however that eventually assured for him a place amongst the immortals of world literature, and what was of more immediate importance to him was that it won for him the special favour of King Sebastian who granted him a royal pension. This, unfortunately, was as irregular in its payments as it was small in size, and with the early death of his royal patron, the popularity of his works began to diminish, with the inevitable result that his broken health, reinforced by poverty, combined to hasten his death. He died in obscure penury in 1580 and it was not until three centuries later that Lisbon realized that she had never raised a monument to her illustrious son. When it was decided to remedy this omission, it was found that no record existed of the site of the pauper's grave. As a result, a mausoleum now stands in the Jeronimo Abbey in Lisbon, destined to remain empty until the 1580 resting place of the neglected Camoens can be identified with certainty.

These views of the Camoens controversy arose

solely from local observations and without reference to those of Professor Boxer which present the most reasonable answer to the question as to whether Camoens ever was in Macao. We therefore close this section with a brief summary of Boxer's views:

(a) The first mention of an association of Camoens with Macao was made, without the production of any proof whatsoever, about a quarter of a century after the death of the poet.

(b) From the early 1600s, most of his biographers repeat the claim that Francisco Barreto — Governor of Portuguese settlements in India from 1555–1558 — sent Camoens east 'either in exile or in a minor official capacity, where he wrote part of his great epic in the [Macao] grotto which now bears his name'. . . . Regarding the details of his service during those years, his residence in Macao, his writing of *The Lusiads* and his shipwrecks, no unanimity of opinion is expressed.

(c) 'No single contemporary book, document or record extant makes an allusion direct or indirect' to Camoens ever having been in Macao.

(d) In his known writings, Camoens never makes mention of Macao, though they 'teem with geographical names and abound in references to places in which he had been'.

(e) The claim was first made in 1613 in Portugal, and it was accepted there as being correct without any critical consideration or observation; it gradually became traditional and as such was later readily accepted in Macao, being first recorded there a century later. With colonial pride and uncritical enthusiasm, Macao accepted the Lisbon story and outshone the motherland with its memorial bust and gardens.

(f) Regarding the grotto, Macao at that time was but a settlement of a few matsheds; it is highly unlikely that a Portuguese would separate himself off from the protection of his fellow countrymen, especially if he was filling an official post requiring his presence in the settlement or on board in the harbour.

(g) While it is romantically satisfying to think of an outcast civil servant as living under such conditions, isolated in a rocky cleft and heroically writing his way back to civilization and worldwide fame, yet the very nature and magnitude of this literary achievement makes the grotto story so much more impossible. *The Lusiads* was a poem of such 'great erudition abounding in classical allusions' that even 'Camoens, classical scholar as he was', needed the facilities far above those that a 'rocky hole' or even the matshed settlement of sixteenth-century traders could supply in Macao. Outside Portugal in those days, these could only be found at Goa.

View of the winding paths in the Camoens Garden, also by George Smirnoff

View of St. Anthony's Church from the Camoens Gardens, by George Smirnoff

São Tiago Fort (St. James), Macao by Marciano Baptista (from the Braga Collection)

The Redoubt of St. Peter, Praia Grande, Macao by George Chinnery

The cloisters of the Seminary of St. Joseph by George Smirnoff

Part of the cloisters of St. Joseph's Seminary by George Smirnoff

Eastern corner of Macao looking south by George Smirnoff

Macao showing Praia Grande Bay from the south by George Smirnoff

Conclusion

THIS BOOK WAS written by two people whose lives were lived in, and in the service of, the British Crown Colony of Hong Kong. Colonialism, the right of one people to rule another, was largely unquestioned in their time. Many of the views implicitly or explicitly expressed in this book are those of the voices of their era. Theirs is a generation for which I feel a very profound respect, and a certain envy too, as in many ways they had the best of the places they lived in. All the same, I am a product of my own life and time, and many of their views are not mine. With this small disclaimer, I have left their conclusions largely untouched.

It is perhaps fitting that this culmination of their life's work should be published in this year of 1999 when, with the retrocession of Portuguese Macao to China, the entire Imperial adventure that began in this region with Jorge Álvares' first landfall in 1513 near Tuen Mun is finally brought to a close. The days that brought forth European colonies on the face of Asia have now passed, and the remarkable group of people who came to these regions have largely passed away, too. We will

never see their like again either in this region or any other, for the world that brought them forth has irrevocably changed.

It only remains to record that the transformation which took place was not all bad — that there was good as well as bad on both sides, and intentions that were noble as well as evil.

The Portuguese presence in Macao, unlike that of the British in Hong Kong, need not be seen — and in many respects should not be seen — as a form of national humiliation to China. They were allowed to settle there in the 1550s, by the consent of the local authorities. This fact has never been questioned. They did not, as did the British, seize a remote corner of the Chinese Empire by force of arms and then settle there by *force majeure*.

True, the Portuguese came to China uninvited. In that respect, they were the same as all other visitors to China from the sea in those far-off days — at the best of times tribute-bearing barbarians, though more usually pirates and sea-robbers with unsavoury intentions. At times their presence in Macao was one that was suffered and tolerated rather than welcomed. Most of the time, though, from the 1550s until the present day, the Portuguese presence in Macao was simply accepted. It was, after all, a little, insignificant place on a remote backwater in the vastness of China, far from centres of power and influence. The occasional, nagging irritation of its strange barbarian presence was tolerated because the annoyance was largely outbalanced by the wealth its trade generated, and because of the knowledge that those strange barbarians could be very easily brought to heel.

When they became too much of a nuisance, the Chinese always retained the whip hand as regards the Portuguese in Macao. Real power, the only type that matters, rested not with the Leal Senado, but with the Mandarin of the Casa Branca, petty official though he was in the Chinese scheme of things. This was the situation, and the Portuguese at Macao knew it. It was only when other European powers forced themselves upon China, demanding recognition of sovereignty over their territory by right, that the Portuguese relationship with the Chinese came onto the same unequal footing that it rested upon with the other European powers in China.

Sovereignty over Macao was not conceded to the Portuguese until 1887, some three hundred and thirty years after they were first allowed to settle there. Even that diplomatic victory, achieved largely with British help, was ultimately a Pyrric one. Portuguese claims to sovereignty over Chinese soil proved to be as transitory as that of all the other territorial claims made upon China in the nineteenth century.

In due course, the Sino-Portuguese Joint Declaration was signed in 1987, after protracted negotiations, providing for the return of Macao to Chinese administration in 1999.

Stone, unlike most other materials, lasts for hundreds, if not thousands of years. Granite reminders of that tremendous and unlikely Lusitanian adventure begun by Prince Henry, the Navigator, in his remote fastness high above the cliffs of Sagres, and concluded on the coast of southern China over five centuries later. It is my hope — and was that of the Rides — that the final echoes of the voices of Macao stones that hint at this whole long saga will continue to resound in quiet corners of Macao for a long time yet to come.

Bibliography

Boxer, C.R. *Macau Na Época Da Restauração (Macao Three Hundred Years Ago)*. Macao: Imprensa Nacional, 1942.

—— *Fidalgos in the Far East 1550–1770*. Hong Kong: Oxford University Press, 1968, c. 1948.

—— *The Christian Century in Japan, 1549–1650*. Berkeley: University of California Press, 1951.

—— *The Dutch Seaborne Empire: 1600–1800*. London. Hutchinson and Co. Ltd., 1965.

—— *The Portuguese Seaborne Empire 1415–1825*. London: Hutchinson and Co. Ltd., 1969.

Braga, José Maria. *The Western Pioneers and their Discovery of Macao*. Macao: Imprensa Nacional, 1949.

Coates, Austin. *Prelude to Hongkong*. London: Routledge and Kegan Paul, 1966.

—— *A Macao Narrative*. Hong Kong: Heinemann Educational Books (Asia) Ltd., 1978.

Fairbank, J.K. Vol. I, 1953.

Legge, James. Vol. I, *Biographical Note by Lindsay Ride*. 1960.

Ljungstedt, Andrew. *An Historical Sketch of the Portuguese Settlements in China and of the Roman Catholic Church and Mission in China*. Boston: James Munroe, 1836.

Macaulay, Rose. *They Went to Portugal*. London: Jonathan Cape, 1947.

Montalto de Jesus, C.A. *Historic Macao*. Macao: Salesian Printing Press, 1926.

Teixeira, P. Manuel. *A Voz das Pedras de Macau*. Macao: Imprensa Nacional, 1980 (in Portuguese).

—— *Toponímia de Macau*. (2 Vols.) Macao: Instituto Cultural de Macau, 1997.

Index